D0447678

Freeing the Human Spirit

The Threefold Social Order,
Money,
and
The Waldorf School

by

Michael Spence

The healthy social life is found
When in the mirror of each human soul
The whole community finds its reflection,
And when in the community
The virtue of each one is living.
— Rudolf Steiner

Published by:
The Association of Waldorf Schools of North America
3911 Bannister Road
Fair Oaks, CA 95628

Freeing the Human Spirit

The Threefold Social Order, Money, and the Waldorf School

Author: Michael Spence

Editor: David Mitchell

Cover Form: Roswitha Spence

Proofreader: Nancy Jane

© 1999 By AWSNA

ISBN # 1-888365-21-8

Table of Contents

Introduction

If it is to fulfill its purpose in accordance with the spiritual reality out of which it teaches, then a Waldorf school must be structured and make its administrative and financial decisions in accordance with that same spiritual reality. Those carrying responsibility for the school - teachers, trustees or board members, and administrators - need to have some understanding of this reality, particularly of the threefold nature of all social and community life. To teach the children on the basis of the reality of the supersensible world and then to work with the money as though no such supersensible world existed is to introduce a dishonesty, a lie, into the life of the school. Such an untruth in the being of the school has its effect and is unconsciously perceived by more people than we may think.

In nearly all the schools I have visited I have seen the dedication and commitment that the teachers bring to their work. They know that the children come through birth from worlds of spirit, that they bring with them their intentions, potentials, and resolves for this life on Earth. This recognition of the reality of the supersensible world is the foundation of their teaching. But too often it seems to be limited to that which goes on in the classroom; it does not reach into the offices, into the meetings, and the working arrangements. This supersensible reality is denied when it comes to dealing with those things of this world, with legal matters, with money, with the fees and salaries. Then, conventional business economic thinking prevails.

If we accept that the spiritual world is a reality, that there are spiritual beings who connect themselves to our work and our institutions, then we must take into account the working of these spiritual beings when we work with such things as money. We must recognize that the way we work with fees and salaries, with decision making and the general structure of a school will have its consequences for the health or ill health of the institution.

I have come to realize ever more strongly that we must strive for an integrity in the totality of the school or other institution. This integrity to the spiritual reality must permeate every aspect of the work. To ignore, for instance, the reality of the threefold nature of social life is to fail to work out of Anthroposophy into the school as a whole. It is not enough to work on the basis of spiritual science in the classroom, but to allow untruths to flourish in the administrative activities of the school. The children themselves will also sense these untruths. I was constantly astonished at the comments made by my children about their teachers and the life of the school. I do not believe that my children were exceptional in this. Although they did not understand the implications of what they saw and of which they spoke, on a deeper level it was clear that they recognized those teachers who worked out of a genuine commitment to Anthroposophy, and those who did not do so. This was despite the fact that they themselves maintained that they disapproved of "Anthroposophy" and wanted the school to be "normal."

When potential parents visit the school, what do they see? What leads them to decide for or against the school for their children? How often, when we later talk to parents and ask them what made them decide to put their child into a particular Waldorf school, do we hear such phrases as: "We sensed that the school was what we had been looking for," or "We felt that the school was the right place for our child." Time and time again one is left with the impression that they did not make their decision only from what they had been told, or by their understanding of the curriculum. There was very often something more, something that could not be consciously defined or grasped.

It is my experience at Emerson that many people visiting the College were able to see more than was outwardly visible. Working as bursar of the College, I have had occasion to meet many people from all walks of life, many with no knowledge of Anthroposophy or the reality of the spiritual world: people from business and industry, representatives of various organizations, local authority officials, tax inspectors, and the police. On many occasions I have been astonished at the comments they have made. It has been quite evident that on an unconscious level they saw or sensed something that was present in the supersensible environment of the College. Many people do have a dim sense of the spiritual basis of an organization, of the spiritual truths or untruths that sustain the whole.

Unfortunately, there is at present widespread confusion concerning the threefold social order. It constantly astonishes me that much of what is said in books, articles, lectures, and discussions concerning the threefold social order bears little relationship either to what Rudolf Steiner said or to the facts of outer reality. Too often such statements are accepted as authoritative, although anyone carefully studying the matter should be able to see that frequently they do not make sense. Rudolf Steiner said that the adverse spiritual powers would try to prevent the threefold social order coming about. I do believe that one of the ways they do this is by sowing confusion through misleading statements. Certain areas of confusion that have arisen will be discussed later in Chapter Two.

A study of the threefold nature of social life can be an immensely rewarding and exciting experience. The more one penetrates into its depths the more one comes to a realization of the great wisdom and artistry that has, throughout the stages of human evolution, brought it into being. It is as though all of Anthroposophy, in all its limitless sweep, when focused not on the individual, but on the wide community of earthly humanity leads us to the threefold social order. In a lecture given in Oxford on 26th August 1922, Rudolf Steiner said:

> . . . But to say how, out of the configuration of our economic life, out of the single concrete facts furnished by nature, by human labor, by the spirit of human discovery and cooperation an existence worthy of the human being is gradually to be produced - that requires a more profound expert knowledge than any other branch of knowledge, any other branch of natural science. For as compared with the complexity of social and economic facts, what we see under the microscope and through the telescope in the heavens is quite simple.

This does not mean that it is too complicated to grasp, or that one needs exceptional powers to understand it. Above all it requires that one have a real interest in social life, an interest that goes beyond the immediate circle of one's own friends and associates, and that one develop powers of uncritical, objective, compassionate observation. This interest in all people and in all human activity is a fundamental requirement for any deeper understanding of the threefold nature of social life. Too often our interests are confined to our immediate circle of friends and work colleagues and to our own selves.

Humanity itself is a "Being," just as the individual human being is. And just as the individual human being has a three-fold nature, or structure, so, too, has earthly humanity a three-fold nature. When we understand and know something of this threefold nature of our social "Being," we will come to know also how to form and structure our individual organizations.

The threefold social order is not a scheme, method, or strategy for forming or running an organization. No prescription as to how to form and run schools in detail can be given. Each school is an individual Being. Just as the reality of the threefold nature of the human being is true for every person we meet but manifests in each differently, so every institution is three-fold in its being, but in each this comes to expression in a different way.

Today money plays a dominating role in human affairs. It takes hold of our three soul forces of thinking, feeling, and willing far more than most of us realize. The way fees and salaries are approached is something that will affect all those involved in the school: teachers, administrative staff, and parents. It will have its effect on the health or ill health of the school itself. In my opinion it is not possible to understand money or to bring a healing to its negative influences on community life except on the basis of an understanding of the threefold social order.

I will go into the question of salaries in some detail. Through a study of salaries we can throw light on many areas, such as the relationship of the individual to the institution, to his work, to personal karma, and to human freedom.

In the first part of this book I will attempt to give an outline of the threefold nature of social life in society as a whole. It is not possible to give more than an outline, but it is my intention that what is given, combined with an active observation of social life, will form a sufficient foundation for further study and for coming to perceive how it manifests in a school.

In the second part I will give some ideas as to how a Waldorf school or other such organization can begin to form itself in accordance with its own nature as an institution within the cultural realm of society. It is not my intention to give any form of prescription or detailed outline of how a school should organize itself on the basis of its threefold nature. No organization can be strong and healthy if it merely follows directions from outside itself. It must come to its own form and structure out of its own struggles and research. Those who form and lead the school must know why they act in any particular way and do so because they themselves have come to know that it is the right way. What I give here is intended to be no more than light thrown on the subject from one particular direction in order to help people see where they are going and where they may want to go.

What I set out in this book comes out of my experience of twenty-seven years as bursar of Emerson College in England, and for most of that time doing research and running study groups and workshops for students, administrators, and teachers on the "Threefold Social Order" and on "money." I had also to make the concepts of the threefold nature of social life the basis of my work in the College in dealing with administrative arrangements and with money. I took it always as a challenge that students and visitors from the world at large should find, even unconsciously, in the practical work of the office something that was founded on the same truths as that which was being taught in the classroom – that there would be no spiritual untruths between that which the College taught and its actions.

Because my experience has been at Emerson College, I will draw on examples of how we have tried to work here. This is not because I think we have any final answers, or are more successful or advanced than other places, but this has been my experience out of which I can speak directly. I also do believe that Francis Edmunds, who founded the College, and John Davy, who also played a very important part in the early formative years, were able to lay into the very being of the College certain concepts and principles that gave it a healthy foundation of a threefold structure that still lives today.

But Emerson deals with adult students. Most of them come for one year, some for two or more. Each year is considered separately. We do not have a parent body. These differences must be born in mind when examples are given. I hope they can be illuminating, but they cannot just be copied.

Today more than ever before, someone writing in English comes up against the question of gender. Whereas it is possible to use such words as "human being" instead of "man," there is no non-gender word for "he," "him" or "his," and to say "him and her" each time is too cumbersome. In the strict sense of the language the masculine can have two meanings, one gender neutral and referring to people of either sex, and the other referring to the masculine. So, in correct English "he" can refer to both male and female, but "she" cannot properly refer to the male. But in this time of the awakening of the human soul to the consciousness of self, this quite understandably does often stir emotions. This is true in some countries more than others. I have decided to use the masculine in the first part of the book. In the second part I will be more particularly addressing those working in the schools, and as these are mostly women, I shall then use the feminine. I hope this will not be too distracting for some people.

PART ONE

Chapter 1

Preliminary Overview

It may be of value to give here something of an overview of the threefold social order. Most of this will be discussed in more detail later.

The most immediate and obvious aspect of the human being is the physical body. This is the first thing we see when we meet another person. By this is meant everything of a person that is made up of physical substance, everything that is subject to the laws of physics - gravity, temperature, etc., and that at death is placed in the grave and returns to nature from which it is derived.

Over against this is all that is variously referred to as soul, mind, psyche, spirit, self, etc. The recognition that social life does have three distinct spheres does not depend on whether a person believes that his "soul" is something of a supersensible nature that continues on after death, or that it is merely an expression of the working of the physical brain and nervous system, like a super computer that ends at the death of the body. What is important is the recognition that every normal human being experiences himself as an "I" who has his or her own feelings, thoughts, desires, and abilities, and an urge to create or achieve something.

Thus, a person experiences a twofold nature within himself: the bodily nature, which can be seen, measured, and understood through the normal physical senses, and the "soul" nature, which cannot be so perceived through the physical senses – that which each individual experiences and can know for himself, but which cannot be directly perceived by another. The needs that arise out of this twofold nature are quite different and distinct.

In general, we can say that the sphere of activity within the social life of humanity that provides for those needs that arise out of the bodily nature of the human being we refer to as the "economic" sphere or sector. That which provides for the needs of what we call the "soul" will be referred to as the "cultural" sphere or sector.

But a human being has a third need. He has to have a "place" within the order of other human beings. He feels that within the community he has rights and should be treated equally with others. Out of this need the sphere of law and the democratic state has arisen. This will be referred to as the "rights" sector or sphere, or the sphere of the "State."

Thus, we recognize that within the life of each individual human being three areas of need arise in relation to the wider social community. The social life of humanity has these three "members" or "spheres," each with a quite different and particular nature and each serving a particular need of the individual human being within society.

14

Three Demands of the Soul

Three social ideals first called forth at the time of the French Revolution and more and more widely striven for today are freedom, equality, and what is variously called mutuality, brotherhood, or community. So long as society is seen as one unitary entity, there will always be a conflict between these three. If all three ideals are striven for, then each will to a certain extent nullify or cancel the others. Only when the three different realms of society are recognized, and each separate realm strives towards a different ideal are the three achievable within the whole.

Three Spheres of Social Life

By "economic" we refer to all human activity that is involved in the production, distribution, and consumption of commodities, not just the activity of making a profit. Between birth and death we inhabit a physical body, and for this we need the transformed substance of the earth, that is of the mineral, plant, and animal kingdoms, and also of the sub nature forces of electricity, magnetism, nuclear energy, etc. If we look at all we have and use during our life time – our house, transport, food, clothing, heat and power, and much else – we will see that it all has its origin in nature; it has been taken from there and transformed by human activity. Of all that we have or use throughout our lifetime, we produce almost nothing by ourselves. We cannot do otherwise. We depend on the work of very many, of countless, other people for what we need. Mutuality or community is the basis of economic life. There, people are not free. No one can live without the basic necessities of life, and no one can produce these entirely for himself. Nor are people equal in economic life. Some need more than others; the weak cannot produce as much as the strong. People have differing strengths and abilities.

In every human being there are anti-social forces. In former times these were largely held in check by the restraining forces of family, tribe, and religion. But these increasingly have lost their power. Social life has had more and more to create structures to restrain or keep back these anti-social impulses. Everything that is established to achieve this as law, regulation, codes of conduct, and agreed behavior is the proper sphere of the rights life, of the democratic administration or government. All those matters within the social structure about which every person's opinion is of equal value and importance are the proper sphere of rights or democratic government. Here it is equality that must hold sway. And equality must not be confused with sameness.

Everything within the social life of the community that works for human development, that nurtures the life of the soul, develops individual skills, searches for knowledge, or fosters the striving for individual achievement and excellence falls within what we refer to as the cultural life of the community. All education, art, religion, science, entertainment, training, etc., belong to this sphere of society. Furthermore, always in everything that touches the single human being from the cultural life of the community the freedom of the individual must be considered as inviolable.

These are the three spheres or realms of social life that in their interweaving, each working according to their own inner law and nature, form the unity of human social life in its unfolding through evolution.

Money plays such a dominating role in our lives today. It is often confused with the economic sphere itself. It is something that has developed a life of its own, and any study of the threefold social order must include some consideration of the place and working of money.

Historical Evolution

Just as the individual human being has evolved out of the past and continues to develop into the future, so humanity itself is a living being that evolves and changes its form out of the past and into the future. Many of the social forms of today are remnants of the past and are no longer appropriate to the present state of human development. There are also those which have to come about in the future but are already present in seed form.

There is not space in this book to go into this in detail, although it does make a very interesting study. I will briefly point to certain developments that are of particular importance for our study.

One that is of particular importance is the change in the relationship of the individual to the group, family, or people into which he is born. In earlier times of human evolution, it was the group that was primary, the group or people connected through a common ancestry, through the blood. The individual within this group was subordinate. It was as a member of the group that he found his purpose and identity; he was one with and of the group and had little consciousness of himself as separate from it.

The group found its purpose and identity in that which came from the spiritual world through the leaders and the initiates, who developed inner powers of clairvoyance and who, through the mysteries, were able to "bring word from God." In this way the guidance for all matters concerning the group was sought and given. This included not only those matters which concerned the inner life of the people, but also all that concerned affairs of law and order and the economic life.

In our time this is no longer appropriate. Now the individual has emerged as an independent being conscious of himself and the "voice" from within. The blood relationship, the family, or tribe must now be subordinate to the individual.

Although even at that earlier time there were the basic elements of the threefold social order, that which later became the rights and economic spheres were contained within what was the forerunner of our present cultural sphere. This was the time of the theocracies. It was not until the Greek and more particularly the Roman civilizations that there arose the consciousness of being an individual, a citizen of the earthly State. Then what was experienced as the divine commandment was no longer felt to answer many of the needs that now arose in the human soul, particularly those questions of relationship between one person and another, between master and servant, and between the single person and the social group. The sense of individual human rights emerged, and man-made laws, as opposed to divine commandment, came into being. So the rights life separated off from the all embracing cultural sphere and developed a life of its own with its own particular nature and thought structure. Thus developed the concepts of the "balance" of the scales in which to weigh good and evil, right and wrong, and of jurisprudence, logic, and dialectic.

It was not until nearer our own time that the economic life separated itself off and became independent of the other two. This started in the fifteenth and sixteenth centuries, but it was only in the nineteenth and the early parts of the twentieth centuries that the independent economic life as we know it today emerged. Born in England in the industrial revolution, the leadership was then taken over by America, which has become the driving force behind it. Now, at the end of the twentieth century, this economic life has developed such independence and power of its own that it has come to dominate the whole of social life and to spread its dominion across all of humanity.

Obstructions to Progress

But economic thinking itself is still dominated by thought forms that rightly belong to the cultural or to the rights spheres of social life from which it has now become separated. The necessary concepts with which to take hold of our complex economic sphere of activity have not yet been found. For example, we see price as fair or just when both sides are in balance, when one value is exchanged for another of equal value. This leads away from a social economics that aims to provide for all; it takes no account of the actual nature of human beings that have different capacities and needs.

Egoism and the principle that every individual should be free to pursue his or her own interests have a proper and necessary place in cultural life. They should have no place in economics, but they have in fact come to dominate economic thinking and activity, where they work with destructive power.

Humanity has not yet developed the necessary thoughts with which to take hold of economic life in such a way that it can serve all humanity. To any objective observation of economic life today it will be clear that it is not under any form of conscious human control. It has taken on a life of its own often guided by spiritual beings working against the rightful course of human evolution.

The actual economic activity of production and distribution has largely been lost sight of, particularly by those who are not directly involved, except as consumers. Money has become a veil that obscures everything that lies behind it. It so dominates our lives that in many ways we are becoming quite unfree, but unaware of the fact.

That is one impediment to the rightful evolution of modern social life – the growing dominion of the economic sphere, or more particularly of money and finance, over the whole of humanity.

Another is our expectations of democratic government. In ancient times people looked up to the initiates, to the priest/kings for direction in all aspects of social life. That was appropriate, when it was the divine creator powers themselves that spoke through the leaders of mankind, when the individual did not have an existence separate from the group. But today we live in an entirely different situation. Yet we continue what was right in the ancient past in that we expect of our now democratically elected leaders the same all encompassing wisdom that could be expected from the initiates in former times. In our thinking we still look to them for the solution of all our social problems.

A further impediment is the emptiness of our present cultural life. It has not kept up with human evolution and is very largely unable to nourish the modern human soul. There is little in it that speaks to the human being of his own true nature, that leads him to any form of existence based on a knowledge of his spiritual origins.

These are some of the unhealthy disorders within our present human social life.

It is not easy to overcome the concepts and ways of thinking that we absorb into ourselves from the social environment in which we live during our growing up and in our adulthood. To come to a working imagination of the threefold social order means first putting aside all our present concepts and ways of thinking that presume a unitary and self contained state with a central government seen as responsible for all aspects of the community social life. To get rid of something so deeply ingrained in our conceptual life and to replace it with the concepts of the threefold society is not easy. In my experience most people try to superimpose the one on the other, and this leads to confusion. The most difficult part is to completely remove the idea of existing government or central authority from one's picture of society.

But in a society or community forming itself on the basis of its threefold nature, the three spheres or domains would each work alongside the other two, no one being dominant. Each would act out of, and be responsible for, those areas that fall properly within its domain. This would include nothing of a central government as we know it.

Many people are discouraged by the thought that there is not much the individual can do, that a threefold society cannot be achieved, the changes needed are just too great, and the present system is too well entrenched. They feel that whatever one does is only scratching the surface. But such thinking is based on a failure to understand that the separating out of the three spheres of social life is something that the evolutionary impulses of our time demand and are themselves working towards, just as the three soul forces of thinking, feeling, and willing are separating off from each other in the individual human being.

If we could develop an imagination, an imaginative picture of what it is that is demanded of our age, just this imagination could work with enormous power. It is the imaginative pictures of that which could come about, that which calls us from out of the future, that can fire the will, and it is movement that is important; that we are moving, even if only slowly, towards that goal is important. That we will not reach it in our life time is not important; it is the fact that we actively do move towards it that is significant, not just for ourselves, but for humanity.

It is also true that there already lives in the unconscious depths of the souls of a great number of people a knowledge of and a yearning for the threefolding of social life. One can perceive this in the underlying causes of much of the social upheavals and unrest of our time. Very often just a small step or gesture in the right direction will meet with a response which may be either positive or negative but which will seem out of all proportion to the action taken.

A study of the threefold nature of social life can be approached on two paths, both of which are important, but some people will find one or the other easier to follow. One is through the head, to endeavor to come to an understanding of it. The other is to develop a feeling for it, a sense of the particular nature, laws, and gesture of each of the three spheres.

Chapter Two

Hindrances and Aids to the Study of Social Questions

Before we go further, a word on the study of social life may be appropriate. It is important first to clear certain areas of confusion that often exist in Anthroposophical circles and which lead people into a strange kind of disorientation. In different forms these misunderstandings are fairly widespread and, in my view, have often been a great hindrance to the development of a threefold social order.

The Confusion between "Social" and "Rights"

One is as follows. When we refer to "the threefold social order," or as I often prefer "the threefold nature of social life," we are talking about the earthly social life of humanity, that is, the human society that the individual enters at birth and leaves again at death. Just as the individual human being has a three-fold nature, so also does this earthly human community as a whole.

The threefold human being consists of body, soul, and spirit. In the threefold life of humanity there are the economic, rights, and cultural spheres. But we cannot simply place the one in direct relationship to the other in an apparently simple, logical order. The reality is much more complex than that.

There is too often a tendency to see one threefold structure as a simple extension of another, to find ways of putting them into charts. This is one source of confusion.

Another, connected to the above, but more complex, is as follows. A symptom is seen when people refer to the rights or middle sphere as the "social" sphere; that is, the three are referred to as:

> the cultural/spiritual sphere,
> the "social" sphere and
> the economic sphere

The rights sphere, or the sphere of the State, of law and politics, disappears and is replaced by the "social" sphere. In all my studies I have never found that Rudolf Steiner spoke of the threefold social order in this way. He has always called that sphere which he usually, but not always, places in the middle, the sphere of rights, of the State, of politics, or some similar term.

As I understand it, the train of thought that leads to this confusion goes something like this:

The human being stands in the middle between the three realms of hierarchies above him and the three kingdoms of animal, plant, and mineral below. He is involved with each of these. The individual strives upward out of the impulses of his soul/spirit nature to the higher hierarchies on whom he depends for his inner development and evolution. This is then perceived as the cultural/spiritual sphere. In his bodily nature he is dependent on the three earthly kingdoms below for sustenance. This is understood to be the economic sphere. Between these two he is in community with other human beings with whom he must find a social relationship. It follows that this is then the rights sphere. But arrived at in this way, the term "rights" or "the State" does not easily fit; it does not ring true. It is then called the "social sphere."

There is a failure to see that it is this "social sphere" that is threefold and that we are referring to when we talk of the threefold social life. It is this sphere of human community, that lies between the realm of the higher hierarchies above and the kingdoms of nature below, that has to become threefold, if it is to fulfill the social needs of human beings.

Of course, there is some relationship between these two threefold structures, but it is no more than that. To understand the relationship one must first see them as distinct. The following diagram will perhaps help.

The Hierarchies

The Human Community → Social life → Cultural
                                        → Rights
                                        → Economic

The Kingdoms of Nature

Failure to make this distinction has led to strange results and widespread confusion. The inability to see that it is the human social realm that has to be made threefold, combined with a common tendency to make diagrams with a logical projection, as mentioned earlier, results in the following distorted picture:

The Hierarchies	→ Cultural/Spiritual		Spirit	Freedom
The Human Community	→ Social		Soul	Equality
The Kingdoms of Nature	→ Economic		Body	Brotherhood

They may not often have actually been described in this way, but it has become a habit of thought in very many people's minds and is clearly the basis on which many lectures and discussions take place. In my observation this way of thinking is more prevalent in England and Europe than in America. It has not been really thought through, or the obviously incorrect conclusions would have been clearly seen. The next step would be that the proper place for democracy is the realm of the soul, so schools should come under the control of the democratic State. But that is clearly not so, and it is never taken that far. People most certainly are not equal in the life of soul, and that makes nonsense of the demand for freedom in education. On the contrary, it is just in the life of soul that freedom must be given, and it is in the Spirit that all people are recognized as equal. The realm of the "State" has disappeared from the picture as clearly the human being cannot give his soul or his spirit nature over to the State.

On several occasions Rudolf Steiner described the economic as the social sphere. I do not know anywhere where he refers to the life of rights as the social sphere.

In this way of thinking the sphere of rights, the realm of the State, is largely hidden, veiled over by a sort of extension of the cultural sphere with attributes of economic life.

But something else is hidden from view, something to which we should be very awake. The sphere of the State, the rights life, is that realm which includes only those things which belong wholly to the life on earth, the life between birth and death. The "usurping Prince of this world" reigns when such an earthly authority tries to use its power to control the cultural sphere, that is, the sphere of the supersensible nature of the human being, or the economic life.

Social - The Individual of Society as a Whole

There is another area of confusion that is sometimes connected to what has just been described. This also revolves round the word "social," which has a very wide meaning.

Here we must distinguish between on the one side all that which concerns a healing of the social life of humanity as a whole, which to a certain extent must include the smaller groupings, such as organizations and institutions, and on the other side all that arises from the individual, who has to take hold of his feelings, thoughts, and actions in order to integrate socially with the people with whom he lives or works in community.

What we refer to as the threefold social order is all that derives from the threefold nature of humanity as a whole. Within this is the cultural realm, which is concerned with that which arises out of the soul life of the human being.

The individual human soul, particularly at this time of the awakening of the consciousness soul, experiences loneliness, being cut off from other people, not being understood, or able to communicate. What is usually meant when people talk of social work is the dealing with the social or antisocial problems of individuals within society. To be active in this area of social work demands powers of perception and understanding of the human being. It demands also an understanding of the working of destiny and karma. By its nature it is work that belongs to the cultural life of the community, just as does that of the teacher, the doctor, and the judge.

The single person finds himself in community with others with whom he has to come into some form of social relationship. Whether it is with another person, or between people within a group, problems frequently arise. Personal interests, individual feelings, and karma are always present and make for social division between people. In a school the work, particularly of the meetings, is often hindered, in fact sometimes made impossible, by such personal clashes or inability to work together. Important as they are, it is not the intention of this book to deal directly or advise on such social questions. There are others much more qualified in such matters than myself. But indirectly, if all those involved and active in the school work out of an understanding of the threefold social order, then it will be seen that such questions do not arise so often or with such force.

The threefold social order concerns itself with the structure and ordering of human society as a whole according to the inherent and evolving nature of human society and its rightful form in our time. When the community, whether of humanity as a whole, or a group or institution within that whole, such as a school, finds its form according to this threefold nature, then each individual within the whole will "feel at home." That is, he will experience that the needs of the individual and of the whole are in harmony, each nurturing and recognizing the other.

So we have the threefold social order, which strives to bring order and health into the community as a whole. Alongside this we have all that social activity which arises out of the needs of the individual. Both are important, but they should not be confused. Rudolf Steiner placed great emphasis on the importance of the threefold social order; he devoted a great deal of his time and energy to the question. He spoke of this as the most important evolutionary impulse of our time. This is what he time and again referred to as "the social question." It must not be submerged and lost sight of behind that which is also a need of so many people today, the quest for a healing of the life of soul, and of the relationship to those with whom a person lives and works.

The healing and nurturing of the life of soul is at the very center of the task of the cultural sphere of the community.

When the word "social" is used for the rights sphere, further confusion is added to what is already confused.

Observation

A practice that is of great importance in trying to come to an understanding of social questions is observation. Though essential as a foundation, it is not enough only to read and study what Rudolf Steiner or others wrote and said. By itself, this will lead to a dogmatism that will have little or no foundation in the reality of social life. To come to any practical understanding of social life, a person must be actually involved in it. Too often people think out social solutions "in the loneliness of their study." In studying social questions this will inevitably lead to false ideas and confusion. Rudolf Steiner points to this fact in, amongst others, the third lecture of *"The Inner Aspects of the Social Question."* True social perception can only be achieved within social life itself, not in isolation.

To do this it is necessary that we develop a real interest in other people – not just those with whom we have some connection, or who are of like nature to ourselves, but those who are different and with whom we have no connection, of whom we might even disapprove and have nothing in common. Only when we put all judgment aside and observe with real loving interest will life itself reveal its true nature to us. Observation of everyday life and of human activity and work, of the work of the waiter in a restaurant, the lawyer in the courtroom, or the performer in a concert hall, whenever we are involved with others, must become something akin to a meditation.

A further aspect of this is to constantly take one's ideas and thoughts out into the street, into the city, the factory, and work place, and there see if they make sense, if they are true to the reality.

This can be a very revealing and enlightening exercise. Take a thought, something perhaps that you have read or in some other way come to or perceived for yourself. Take it out into everyday life, out "into the street." There, perhaps in the market place or shop while you are buying something, or when you stop to watch some building works, or when sitting in a restaurant or concert hall, bring up your ideas and offer them to the situation. To do this it is essential that you put aside all your own opinions, judgments, and subjectivity, that you fully observe and take a loving interest in all that is around you. If you do this regularly, you will be surprised how your powers of observation develop, and how, with growing clarity, the situation speaks to you, confirming or otherwise, the validity of your ideas, and even reveals something of itself in answer to a question that you have carried within you.

The involvement and real interest in all that goes on around us, without the judgment which so often we place between ourselves and those before us, is an essential foundation for such an exercise.

Later in this book, particularly in Chapter Seven, I discuss the polarity between work that is done because it is one's own work, work that one wants to do out of one's own pre-birth resolves and which brings fulfillment to oneself, and other work that is done because it is needed by others, that brings no inner soul nourishment and is done because it is "paid for." As I shall show in more detail later, cultural and economic activity each lie at opposite ends of this polarity.

It is very important for any understanding of the three-fold nature of social life that this polarity be seen and understood. But it cannot be grasped by thinking and study alone. That will always lead to concepts unconnected to social reality. Social questions can only be grasped by observation from within social life itself. To do this it is necessary to put aside all one's own preconceptions, to leave everything of one's own behind, and just observe the person working. It does, of course, require practice.

For example, when listening to a professional musician giving a performance, observe the situation closely, observe it as a meditation. Leave everything of yourself aside, all personal feelings, beliefs, and assumptions. Allow only that which is happening before you to speak. Try to live into the creative process, into the activity of interpreting and creating the music that is resounding in the space around you. Then bring before yourself as questions the two possibilities: the impulse, the necessity, that impels the individual to create such music can come from outside - the need to earn money – or it can come from an inner impulse, a need of the soul to create music. Would the music be the same in either case? Each of us needs to find our own way into such questions.

In the same way one can observe the work of the person at the check-out at the supermarket, the policeman controlling the traffic, or the factory worker. It makes an enormous difference if these questions are asked in the actual situation, after one has really taken time to live into what is happening, or if they are asked in the separateness of one's own study. In the actual situation you will come to experience that the situation itself speaks to you, reveals something of itself to you.

There is yet another kind of observation that is necessary, if we are to understand how the spirit world helps or hinders the affairs of human beings within social life. One way to do this is to learn to observe what happens after one or another decision has been made. For example, as a school develops, it will at times have to take on an additional teacher. It may well be that such a decision is only made when there is clearly enough income to pay the costs. But there may come a time when, for one reason or another, there is such confidence in a person, a sense that that person's destiny lies with the school, that it is decided to take him or her on to the staff, although it is not clear how the extra costs are going to be met.

In such situations it is important that we develop the necessary powers of observation in order to perceive what happens within the school as a whole over a period of time after the one decision and after the other. Of course, we have to do this often. We must get beyond what may be considered as chance or coincidence. Then we may come to perceive that there is a response to our work from the spiritual world, that our decisions are not matters that only concern us on earth. We will come to understand something of the nature of the spiritual background to our actions.

A further example: Can we actually observe the change that takes place when a group of colleagues who carry the work of a school are able to transform their thoughts, the concepts that live in them, and that are there behind the structure of the school and the decisions? This is especially pronounced when one that is untrue, that does not reflect reality, is replaced by one that is true. For instance, it is very common to think in terms of the fee the parents pay as being a purchase, a buying of education. Though it may be understood by all in the school that education cannot be bought and sold, that the fee is actually a kind of gift, the reality is often that they still think and act as though it were a purchase. It is the concepts that form the basis of our actions that are decisive. The actual thoughts and concepts that are present when fees are discussed with parents, when "scholarships" are given, or funds set up to help parents meet the fees - the cost of the education - are too often based on the concepts of purchase and sale, of that which belongs only to economic life. That these are untrue concepts for education will be shown later in this book.

If the teachers and other staff members are able to transform their actual thinking, the basic concepts upon which they act, to ones that are true, they will observe a remarkable change in the life forces, in the well being of their school.

We need to develop powers of observation to see these things, to know the deeper consequences of our actions, and of the spirit that is there involved in all our earthly affairs. We need to sense when there are untruths within the Being of the school, to ferret them out and work on them.

Chapter Three

Cultural Life

The Stars spoke once to Man
It is World Destiny
That they are silent now,
To be aware of the silence
Can become pain for Earthly Man.

But in the deepening silence
There grows and ripens
What man speaks to the stars.
To be aware of the speaking
Can be strength for Spirit-Man.
— Rudolf Steiner

A school or college is an institution whose work lies in the cultural sphere of society. The recognition of the nature and inner laws of cultural life will help those who work in the school to find their social form and healthy way of working.

Today there is little in life that speaks to the human being of his own true nature. The development of natural science, the rise of the industrial and later the financial domains that have spread across the world from the west, have also put their stamp on the prevailing concept of the human being. Education is largely based on the idea that he is something not very different from a super computer that has to be programmed. We are constantly bombarded from all sides with the thought that there is nothing more to the human being than what arises out of his bodily nature, like the "characteristics" or "soul" of a machine or computer, and that the human body is only a more advanced and complex form of what modern science develops as machines, systems, substances, and products in economic life. This picture of the human being can be recognized as underlying much of education in all parts of the world. It is what is constantly pressed onto us by commercial advertising and in television, particularly in the science, nature, and school programs, and can even be found as the basis for much of today's religious thinking.

Is there nothing more to human life than we are in this way led to believe? There are many people who do think there is something more, something of a moral, supersensible nature. But how and where to find it? These are central questions of cultural life.

Life itself points to the reality of something more than what can be explained only on a material level. Most people when they were young had questions concerning the meaning and purpose of life and of their own true nature. But they found no answers in their education, nor in what science or religion had to give, not answers that spoke truly to the questions arising out of their own inner depths. So then they forgot their questions and now take from life what they can. The young of today find themselves on the same path, though many of their questions are more urgent.

The greatest need of today is the bringing to life all that belongs to the cultural sphere of humanity. Only out of a developed life of soul can the creative imagination, the will, and the moral forces arise that alone can tackle the questions of our society today: the unemployed, the wasting environment, the strife, and the dispossessed, and the soul emptiness of existence for so many millions of people.

It is not sufficient for people just to have work in order that they can earn their wages or salary. There is a purpose in life on earth other than this. Strong in the human soul is the need to develop itself and its own soul powers, to develop courage, creativity, compassion, and love, and to accomplish those tasks that it has resolved to realize while on earth.

Individual Impulses and the Purpose of Life

If we listen to or read with deep loving and tender interest the biographies of people, of their hopes, intentions, and ambitions, of their trials, sufferings, and successes, and of what led them into their particular course of action, work, or life style, it will become clear that every human being is unique and individual. We will also become aware that their lives were not haphazard series of events, but that there was a definite impulse or intention that led them to do what they did, some driving force that impelled them to follow a certain path and way of life. In some people this is very clear; in others it is not at all obvious, but it is there to be seen in every human life if we delve deeply enough.

Every human soul, often hidden in the depths of its being, brings to earthly life either one or both of two tasks: one to achieve something of his own development, the other to achieve a particular task for the benefit of others or of humanity itself. This is most easily seen in young people, though now all too often modern education and the thought forms induced by economic life so smother it that it cannot come to life.

In so far as a person does find his true place and work in life, he is fulfilling his own pre-birth resolves. He is doing what he prepared himself to do while still in the spiritual worlds between death and a new life. Then he will find meaning and purpose in his work. In no other way can he find this. In so far as he is in his proper place, a teacher teaches because that is his or her work; it comes out of individual destiny and karma.

In our time and increasingly in the future, in everything that concerns the life of soul, all forms of outer authority must fall away. In earlier times the Gods, the spiritual beings guiding humanity, spoke through the leaders of the people and gave to them the law and instructions how to bring order into the social fabric of the group, when and how to act. In our time the spiritual world no longer speaks to humanity in this way, from above, from outside. Any authority that now speaks from outside or above can only be one speaking out of the past, or one that is an earthly authority, not one of the spirit.

The authority arising out of the democratic process has a proper place in the rights sphere of social life, as does the group of people working in association in economic life. But these forms of authority have no place in cultural life, in that which serves the supersensible in the human being. In cultural life the only authority that an individual can justly recognize is, firstly, that which he comes to out of himself, out of his own experience in life, his own faculties and powers of perception, what he has verified for himself in his own research into life, and secondly, that which he himself recognizes in another person as valid, based on a recognition of the capacities, experience, and destiny of that other.

That which now speaks from out of the spiritual worlds can only do so through what each person can hear speaking to him from within himself through the inner strivings of the soul, and through the impulses and tasks each soul brings with it through birth from out of that spirit world. We have to learn to listen to our own inner voice and that of each other.

But in order to have the firm ground on which to stand in freedom from outer authority, the human being must first awaken his inner self, come to know his own destiny task. He must develop the ears to hear that which speaks to him from within himself.

This awakening of, and listening to, in freedom, what speaks from the depths of human souls through their individual capacities and destinies, through their tasks and impulses, is what gives to the work of the cultural realm its life, its purpose, and its orientation. The artist strives to bring to artistic expression something that wells up in his soul. In so far as he is a true artist he works and creates out of that which he brought as seed, from before birth, and which now he strives to bring to flower. The teacher, too, works out of his own karmic impulses and also of those of the children, who have come to him out of their individual destinies.

The teacher must learn all he can of the technique of teaching, of the stages of child development, of the subject matter of the various classes, etc. But if this is not founded on his own destined task to teach, then it will become mechanical. Nor will he then recognize each individual child and know how to work with him or her.

The most pressing task for all those who work in cultural life is to awaken to the working of karma and destiny, to what each person bears within him as capacity and insight into his life's work. Can we really develop the ability to recognize in our colleagues that he or she is in that particular work because karma has placed him there, that he has in conjunction with the destiny of the school taken on a particular task, that there is a wisdom working in the situation? Can we then have such confidence that we free the situation for that task to be fulfilled for which destiny has placed him there?

This is one aspect of cultural life.

The Wider Task of Cultural Life

As we will see later, cultural life can exist, and those who work in that sphere are free to do so, because there are other people who work in economic life and produce there the material goods and services that the cultural worker needs. To work at a machine in a factory, on the floor of a superstore, or inputing into a computer in an office nearly always means that the worker receives nothing of a soul nourishing nature from the work. He has to let his higher self go to sleep. In this the economic worker has to give up something of his own inner spiritual awakening, so that the cultural worker can awaken to his. This is one aspect of why brotherhood is called for in economic life.

Just as cultural life receives from the economic sphere that which it needs of the material products, so it in turn must provide the nourishment of the soul needed by those who work in economic life. It has a responsibility to so. A similar relationship exists between the cultural and the rights spheres.

The cultural sphere of social life must speak to all of humanity. Those whose work places them in the cultural life have a task and responsibility, whether as teachers, artists, priests, scientists, architects, or doctors, to bring into everything they achieve or create that which nourishes the life of the soul and which can lead every human being to a recognition of his own true nature, to a perception of himself as a being of body, soul and spirit. All art, science, and religion are different viewpoints speaking to the human soul of the same deeper truths of existence. Through this each human being can come to know himself and to "remember his task." Each can then also awaken to that which is moral in life and, thus, to his own individual responsibilities.

To accept that the paying over of money absolves this responsibility is to look only on the surface of life. This should become clearer as we proceed through this study.

Cultural Life Taken Over by Economic Life

Today cultural life is struggling for existence. One of the chief causes of its impotence is that it has to a very large extent been taken over by economic thought forms. If we look at modern everyday social life and ask what is now the driving force behind human activity, we will see that whereas in the ancient past it was "the divine will," today it is "money." For the vast majority of people the urge to earn money has become the main or sole motive and meaning of life. That life on earth has another purpose has largely been lost sight of, though there are signs that a growing number of people are beginning to suspect that there is something more.

All activities such as artistic creativity, teaching, architecture, healing, entertainment, and science have a purpose in themselves; the activity itself brings fulfillment of soul that the money earned through them cannot provide. All this seems to have been more and more forgotten. Cultural life today is such that the human soul is often too weak to resist the temptation of immediate pleasure that the possession of money can bring. It is unable to come to a true evaluation of the profound sense of fulfillment that working out of the deep resolves of the soul can give. A person's achievements in working to fulfill his life's task are taken through death into the future. The money we leave behind.

The human soul has a great need to be challenged, to have to exercise its capacity for initiative, creativity, and courage and to bring something new into being. It wills to awaken its latent powers of imagination, inspiration, and intuition, even if unconsciously. But where in today's world is it to find itself challenged in this way? There are few opportunities in our cultural life that provide the opportunities and challenges needed.

If we look to see where people now go to look for work that is challenging, creative, and exciting, we will see that they go not into cultural life but into the economic and financial spheres, into management of companies and corporations, into creating and marketing new products, both actual and financial, and into the markets buying and selling. That much of this might be socially or environmentally harmful is not the point here; it challenges the capacities of the individual in a way that little else does today. Study the lives of the leaders and the entrepreneurs of economic and financial enterprises. There will be seen individuals of enormous capacity, of great ability of soul.

Not only at the level of the top management of companies, but the young person on the floor of the stock exchange or the futures market, or in front of his several computers, has to develop powers of intuition, to develop a sense for the market. He has to make decisions involving very large sums of money within seconds. He cannot turn to his books of reference or his calculator. He must "know."

Furthermore, he needs the courage to back his judgment with an immediate decision and then to accept the consequences if he got it wrong. But why does all this creative capacity and initiative find its way into economic life, why so relatively little into cultural activity? Abilities in this field of activity can and are measured by the money each earns.

But can the real abilities of the teacher be truly judged by the money he earns, by the salary he is paid? Most teachers, although many on one level know better, do have an underlying feeling that their value is according to what they are paid for their work. This is true even in many Waldorf Schools. This way of thinking is very strong in society today; it arises out of economic thinking. No distinction is made between that which one does because the necessity to do it lies, in the first place, within oneself, and that which is done because the product of the work is needed by others, where there is little or no soul nourishment in the activity itself. Increasingly we think of the work of cultural life, of education, the arts, etc., as producing "products" in the same way as economic activity produces products, and of being able to buy and sell these products as we do those of economic production. So long as we think in this way, we will never understand, nor bring to life, the cultural sphere of society.

It might help here to illustrate this with an example.

Can Education Be Purchased?

We will look at two activities that are in reality fundamentally different but are treated as though they are the same. I will compare two very simple examples, one to illustrate something of economic life and the other, cultural life. In what might appear to be over simplistic examples it is often possible to see clearly what is also true but not so easily seen in more complex situations.

Imagine that a person needs some money. He decides to cook twelve pies and to sell them at a market stall. We can imagine the process – he must first acquire all the materials, then prepare, mix, and cook them. This involves a certain amount of work. When finished, he takes the products of his work to market. There he has the twelve pies on his stand. Someone comes along and buys one. The baker gives him the pie, and the buyer hands over the money, say $5. There is an actual exchange, a pie for $5. The baker then has only eleven pies left, but now he also has $5 in his tin. And so it continues until he has sold them all, until there are no pies left. But the baker now has $60. When the next person arrives hoping to buy a pie, they are all gone, there is nothing left, and he has to go hungry.

Here we see sale and purchase within economic life. There is an actual exchange. Each party hands something over; each parts with ownership but gains ownership of something else, something that is of more value to him than the thing which he gave over. This is true of both parties to the transaction. Imagine now someone is going to give a lecture. There is a charge of $4 for every person attending it. We will assume this is the amount that goes to the lecturer, ignoring any charge there might be for maintaining the hall, etc. What is the nature of this charge? Is it a purchase in the same sense as the charge for one of the pies?

Is there an exchange? The listener will hand over the $4, but does he actually receive anything "in exchange"? It cannot be said that he receives the knowledge "in exchange" in the same way as the pies are exchanged for money. The speaker does not hand over the lecture, or a part of the lecture, nor the knowledge. He does not himself know less, or have less knowledge at the end of his lecture than at the beginning. On the contrary, most speakers find that they actually gain in the speaking. Nor will there come a time when it has all been bought, and there is nothing left for the next person. It is often difficult to lecture to a small audience of only a few people. The lecture itself will improve, and everyone will benefit when more listeners come in. We cannot say that there is a given amount of knowledge that has to be shared out, and the larger the audience, the less each receives.

The speaker, if he is in his rightful activity in accordance with those impulses that he carries within himself, like the artist, will actually need an audience. He finds the fulfillment of his work, his creativity, in their interest in what he has to say. One could even think that the lecturer should pay the audience; he needs them to listen to him just as much as they need him. The teacher needs the children; it is the fulfillment of a destiny responsibility.

So what is the nature of the payment? It is clearly not an exchange. Almost everything that applies in the case of the pies is actually the opposite here. In the case of the lecturer we can not truthfully speak of a "purchase." To call it so merely leads to an untrue understanding of the real nature of the transfer of the money. Nor can we say it is a purchase of time. In reality it would be more correct to call it a gift, or contribution. It is a contribution that frees the lecturer to do something that he wills to do anyway.

Of course, in this case the baker might well get some enjoyment or fulfillment out of his work. But that can hardly be the case of someone, for example, working in a factory making electric light bulbs or parts for motor cars. Here we are touching on something that is also important in developing a sense for the cultural life of society. This is the polarity that exists between the economic and cultural spheres.

The Two Motives to Work

Unlike the person who, for example, makes electric light bulbs, the teacher or lecturer, in so far as he is in his rightful work, will have come to it out of his own soul impulses, out of his pre-birth resolves. If this is not so, then he will not be able to bring the necessary creativity and imagination to his work.

The vast majority of people find no satisfaction in doing nothing. They have a need to be creative, to teach, paint, design new buildings, invent new ways of making things, or to understand the secrets of nature. Their inner soul impulses lead them to their work. Some of these find themselves in the fortunate position where their capacities are so valued that others are willing to contribute to enable them to work with those "gifts." For them any money they "earn" through doing this work actually frees them to do it, to do what they need to do anyway. Otherwise, they too would have to do their share of economic production, to work in the shared activity of division-of-labor, or in the rights sphere; they would have to find their work out of the needs of the human community rather than out of their own inner impulses. What they receive actually frees them from this; they receive the products of the labor of others but give nothing "in exchange." That which they do is valued in quite a different way. The money they are given is of the nature of a gift, or contribution.

It is vitally important that we see clearly the difference between the two situations in the above picture. Almost everything in modern life, in the customary thinking and assumptions of our time, tends towards casting a veil over this difference.

These are the two fundamental motives that lie behind all work. They are two poles of our social life, just as there are two poles of a magnet. Though in almost all work both are to be found, one is always the primary impulse or motive.

One arises, in the first place, out of egoism, out of the need to give meaning and purpose to one's own life in the fulfilling of one's own destiny. At this pole is all work and activity that arises out of one's own soul needs, one's own karma. It includes all work that goes to make up the cultural life of the community.

The other is where the work comes about through the needs, not of the one doing the work, but of humanity. It is part of world karma that a person is called to work in a factory making motor cars or electric light bulbs. There he produces what is needed by others. Humanity at this stage in its evolution needs such products; that is the motive for the work, not an inner personal need as in cultural activity. This is the basis of economic activity where altruism or mutuality are a primary demand.

What is essentially important here is that those who work in cultural life come to recognize that they are doing what lies in their own destiny. To approach their work as though they are doing it for the money is a denial of this, and it will actually effect the work. It will mechanize it. The money they receive can only truly be something that actually frees them to do what lies in their own necessity. If they did not receive it, they would have to find some other work, probably in economic life.

All the creativity, entrepreneurial and organizational skills, and inventive genius of those who initiate, manage, and develop economic life are first of all born in the cultural sphere. But though these capacities arise and are nurtured there, they enter into the economic life and there have to follow and obey the laws and nature of the realm of economic productive activity. The individual who works in these capacities in economic life cannot be free as one who works in cultural life.

In the same way the development of the feeling for rights and the democratic process, the ability to sense what lives as common opinion in the community, can only arise within a healthy and strong cultural life.

The quality, conduct, and management of both economic life and the rights life are dependent on the health and quality of cultural life.

Chapter Four

The Rights Life
The Realm of the State

    ... And if you follow this thought right through, you come to see that the State represents the exact opposite of the supersensible life. And it is the more complete in its own way, this State, the more fully it fills this opposite role: the less it claims to incorporate in its own structure anything that belongs to supersensible life, the more it merely embodies purely external relationships between one person and another - those wherein all people are equal in the sight of the law. More and more deeply is one penetrated by this truth: that the fulfillment of the State consists precisely in its seeking to comprise only what belongs to our life between birth and death, only what belongs to our most external relationships.

The Inner Aspect of the Social Question
        – Rudolf Steiner

The rights sphere of a community is that in which, out of the feelings, the common opinion of all its members' order is established. This "rights" sphere should only concern itself with those matters in which every person's opinion is of equal importance.

There was a time when there was no earthly or man made law. The further back in human evolution we look, the more we find that it was the divine word, the divine commandment, given through the great teachers of humanity, through the prophets or the mystery centers, that brought order into the outer affairs of human society. But in the course of evolution this gave way to other different forms.

One development was the paternalistic society. This, or some form of it, is still to be found in many parts of the world. Here the leader is seen as a father or mother figure, a head of the family who had the care and ordering of all the members of the "family." He represented or was the mouthpiece of God, and his word was the law. Even now, in our modern democracies we carry a faint remnant of this in that we still look to our leaders, our prime minister or president, to be a kind of all wise father or mother figure.

Through the course of human evolution this ability to reach to the world of Spiritual Beings for guidance faded. As the Divine Commandment came to have less and less power and influence over people, a new earthly law came into being, one formed by human beings themselves, and the concept of the "State" emerged. This is sometimes seen as "God on Earth" and sometimes as the "realm of the Usurping Prince." This law has become, though arbitrary and inadequate, all that humanity now has to bring order or control into social life. Divine or moral law carries little weight with people today; the forces of egoism are far too strong. The alternative is anarchy.

The existence of modern theocratic states does not contradict this. They try to maintain a society through enforcing old doctrines given in earlier ages, instead of forming new human ordinances. They cannot provide the outer social environment needed for that which must be developed in our time, the consciousness soul.

Law as a Limit to Anti-Social Behavior

There are people who would never act anti-socially towards members of their own family or close community, such as stealing from them, but who would quite happily do so to others with whom they have no such connection. Whatever it is that prevents them acting in this way towards their family and friends is missing in their feelings towards others. All of us have something of this anti-social nature within us. That control or constraint which cannot be provided by people's inner discipline is provided for by an outer State, by law, and the enforcement of law.

In this area of social life is all that relates to the establishing of rules, regulations, and law. The law in a particular community can be an expression of that which is felt as right moral behavior, of a sense of what is just and equitable. The law so arrived at in one country or community may be quite different from that in another; different peoples feel differently.

Laws are established by the State. Within organizations, institutions, and smaller communities, other forms of "law" are arrived at, such as rules, customs, conventions, traditions, standards of social behavior, and mutual agreements.

The State has to bring order into social life where that order cannot be arrived at through people's normal individual behavior or moral self discipline. It has to counter the egoism of the individual, where that egoism is destructive to the interests of others, where the majority feeling within the community is that such behavior is anti-social and not to be allowed. For example, we have to bring order into the driving of vehicles along the roads. They must stop at a red traffic light and only go when the green light shows. Similarly, questions of health and hygiene in the work place, or of the handling of food commercially, must be decided and the necessary laws enacted to ensure the agreed standards are maintained. In this area the law must apply to all people equally. If there are exceptions, such as the police or fire engine going through the red traffic light, it is because everyone recognizes and accepts that this is necessary and for the benefit of the community.

The Working of Law - an Example

A small group of people working or living together may decide on a set of rules or guidelines for the conduct of their social behavior or for the efficient running of their joint work. It might well be that these are agreed at a meeting, and that the group is small and closely knit enough that it is not thought necessary to write them down as rules, or if they are written, it is as a record of the discussion. If and when there is a dispute, the original agreement will be seen as a guideline, not an absolute that must be obeyed. The group will base the resolution of the dispute on the present circumstances and the personalities involved but take into account what was originally agreed as guidelines. That or something similar is workable in a small group where everyone is personally connected to everyone else. At this level, however the dispute is resolved, it remains at a human level, even if that means bad feelings between two people. But as the group gets larger, it becomes more and more difficult to work in this way. When it gets to the size where people cannot all know each other, where it is not possible for a person to hold a picture of the whole in his consciousness, then it becomes necessary for rules to be decided by a smaller group acting as representatives of the whole. These agreed upon rules will have to be written down. Then what happens is that it is not the agreement that people have come to but the written word that becomes the law. This is a very crucial point, because it is now that the law becomes dehumanized, or inhuman. When sometime in the future there is a dispute, it is the written law that must be studied to determine the offence. The law lies in the particular words used and in the meaning of those words. In dealings between people it is always possible to find compromise, flexibility, or some sort of understanding, even if it is only in the inability of a particular person to understand the situation and be flexible. That is human. But between people and the written law there can be no human understanding or flexibility. What is written is absolute. One can only try to find ways of interpreting the words in a different way, or even to find some meaning in the words that was perhaps not intended by those who formed the law. In this way one gets round the law. In this way it is also possible to manipulate the working of the law by interpreting the words in different ways, by twisting other meanings out of them.

In the human soul this is experienced as sharp contrast to what was experienced as the divine commandment emanating from an all caring creator.

Setting the Boundaries to Economic Life

As will be seen later, when we consider economic activity in order that creativity, invention, and entrepreneurial initiative can enter into the productive process, at a certain level egoism has to be given entrance into economic life. But this egoism, though a necessary foundation to cultural life, works destructively in the economic sphere, if it is not kept within certain boundaries. This egoism is not itself able to put bounds on itself, certainly not in the present state of human evolution. The necessary boundaries must come from outside the economic domain, where the egoism will become personal interest; it must come from that sphere where every person has an equal voice in the forming of the community.

Some examples of the main "boundaries" that rights life must place around economically productive activity are:

> 1) The amount of human labor to be available within the community for economic production, and the conditions and contractual arrangements of that labor.
>
> 2) Limits to the effect on the natural and social environment of economic activity.
>
> 3) Establishing the basis for ownership, and defining what can be owned privately and what belongs to the community.
>
> 4) The extent to which natural resources, including land and raw materials, are made available for economic production.

These will become clearer when we study the economic sphere.

The idea that "management" can or should establish these boundaries is entirely unrealistic. To say that they have a moral duty is to fail to understand human nature and the necessary working of egoism. Only a rights life that is independent of economic life can do this.

Ownership

Ownership is something that exists only to the extent that rights life establishes it in law. On what basis are things owned? This has varied through the ages and still does so in different countries. In some earlier communities there was no such thing as ownership. The laws of ownership have been variously formed out of usage, custom, and ancient common law. To what extent is ownership valid in terms of all that can be "owned"?

If a person makes something through his own labor or activity, then it is justified that it belongs to him, that he owns it. If he gives or sells it to another person, the ownership will pass to that other person in accordance to the law of that community.

But in most countries it is possible to own other things where the ownership does not have such a foundation. The most obvious example is the ownership of land. In this case ownership does not originate in someone producing the land through his own labor. In almost all parts of the world ownership of land can be traced back to conquest, to the use of force of some kind. That which is first conquered is later sold. But it is only possible to buy or sell land after "law" has been instituted and has established that what is first acquired by force is "owned." To own something means that a person has a right to hold, use, or dispose of it as he wishes and in so far as is allowed by the law. When it is sold, it is this right that is passed over to the purchaser.

Here we now have something that is a "right" established by law being bought and sold in the same way as the product of a person's labor. Something of the consequences of this will be looked at in Chapter Seventeen when we look at salaries.

Another aspect of "ownership" that has very considerable consequences is that in most countries it is, with certain exceptions, always the owner who has the full power over the use and disposal of what is owned. One sees this very markedly in the fact that it is the owners of the shares of a business or factory who, by the fact of their ownership, have ultimate control and are entitled to any profits. They have this, not because they have in any way benefited or put anything into the business, but because they have purchased shares. The money they paid for the shares in most cases did not even go to the business but to the person who sold them the shares. The people whose work generated the profits and also enabled the business to expand were also the ones who gave the shares their monetary value. But they have no such control. They can all be brushed aside. They are entitled to none of the profits, except by the gift of the owners. One might well ask, why does the law give the owner such power, and not, for example, the one who does the work? This is part of the nature of the rights sphere as it exists today.

The question of "ownership," its purpose, meaning, and place in human evolution and its consequences for human society is something that needs further study. In the lectures *The Inner Aspect of the Social Question,* Rudolf Steiner points to the fact that ownership is something that belongs to the rights sphere, to the life between birth and death, to the life on earth. It has no counterpart in the spiritual world.

It is necessary to indicate these questions here, but it would take us too far outside the scope of this book to look into them in detail. The question of the ownership of what is actually a "right" is of major importance in solving so many of the problems of our social life today. It is a question for the rights sphere, not the economic sphere.

Equal Opinion

A help in understanding the nature of rights life is to develop a sense for the difference between two areas in the forming of judgment, two origins of opinion. On the one side are all those matters where value or weight is given on the basis of the expertise, experience, or individual capacity and insights of the person giving the opinion or judgment. One would go to the experienced teacher to know something of the educational needs of a child, but to the doctor for medical advice.

On the other side, and quite different, are those areas of social life where the capacity or expertise of the individual is irrelevant, where all that is important is that it is the opinion or judgment of an individual member of the community. For example, in a community should certain kinds of theft be regarded as a serious or a minor crime, or even a crime at all? This is a matter on which every person in that community should have an equal voice. The rights life of a community, its laws and regulations, should be an expression of that which arises out of the sum of the individual opinions and feelings of its members, out of the common opinion.

Thus, all questions relating to the life of the soul, to the supersensible in the human being, all that belongs to the cultural sphere of society, except for such matters as the preservation of individual freedom, must be excluded from the domain of the sphere of rights. It must also exclude all matters pertaining to the economic sphere of activity, except for such matters as the establishing of boundaries within which economic life can act for the benefit of society as a whole. The dominion of the State must be confined to those areas of activity where the democratic process is appropriate. But in our life today laws are too often arrived at, not as an expression of what is felt to be right or just within the community, but out of cultural, or more often economic interests, needs, or pressures.

Just as rights life must not be allowed to influence or encroach into either the cultural or economic spheres, so also they must not be able to influence that which is the proper task of rights life.

Equality Is Not Sameness

No two people are the same. If we look at any two people, we see the difference between them. This is particularly obvious if they are of different sexes and of different nationalities and color. They are different; it may even be difficult to find anything that is the same in them. Although in other areas of social life we must recognize the unique and individual nature of each person we meet, in the sphere of the State that must be put aside; there we have to see people as equal, not the same but equal.

Much of the harmful effects of what today is termed "political correctness," arises out of the failure to distinguish between equality and sameness. To treat two people as the same can be experienced as a denial of their individuality and can be debilitating. The seeing of that which is truly equal in them can be experienced as uplifting.

An exercise that can be very helpful is as follows: First, quite objectively and without judgment, observe the differences between two or more people. Then, quietly and with real loving interest in them, ask oneself the question: "Although these two people are quite different and in each I can respect and admire or dislike what is individual and particular, what is it in them that makes them also equal, something that lies beyond that which differentiates?" The answer to this question, in so far as it applies to the outer social life that is lived here on earth between birth and death, leads us to a recognition of the sphere of "rights," to the proper realm of government.

The Separated State

One of the difficulties of coming to an imagination of the threefold social order is the problem of imagining away the present form of one all embracing government. We are so used to the concept of such a government to which we look for the solving of all social problems, including those within cultural and economic life, that it is hard to envisage one that does not go beyond what is indicated as the rights life within a threefold social order. To do this we have to imagine away everything with which the "state" today concerns itself that is actually not within the rightful domain of a democratically elected government. What would it be left with? Almost everything that at present gives it power would be removed from its control.

We have a natural tendency to look to the "government" to deal with matters such as education, health, the environment, the quality of life, poverty, and the unemployed. We see an all wise Prime Minister, President, or other elected leader and his cabinet. For the righting of almost all social problems from poverty, unemployment, poor education, the decline of the arts, the health service, and maintenance of the roads to pollution and provision for the aged, we automatically look to the government – "Why don't they do something about it?" We assume they have the all embracing wisdom to decide on all questions, that they have the wisdom that in earlier times was to be found only in the prophets, in the representatives of, or those appointed by,

God. But have they? Then such individualities truly did have great powers and wisdom; they were endowed by God. Today that is not so; they are individuals of the age of the consciousness soul, elected by the democratic process. They have no special wisdom over all matters.

We have to find a form of social structure that is realistic and appropriate for the people of today, for people of the consciousness soul. What we do have is a caricature of the past, of a theocracy. Only a social structure that is a unity formed of the three separate and independent strands or sectors will meet the needs of the humanity of our time. Each sector must have its own independent organs of "government."

If we really think through what it means when we say that the rights life can concern itself with only those matters where each person's opinion is of equal value or importance, then we will understand how the rights state can only be one that strives to form the community laws and structure according to what lives as feeling for community within the members of that community. This applies whether we are concerned with the rights life of a community, institution, country, or of humanity itself. There must be no question of economic or cultural interests having an influence on such matters.

Let me give an illustration from when I was an elected member of the local parish council. A question came before the council whether a licence should be given to the new owners of a shop to enable them to sell alcoholic drinks. This shop was just outside the local junior school. After some discussion the basic question was considered to be: "What sort of community environment does the local population want?" Did they want the sort of community where alcohol was available just outside the junior school, or did they want their children protected from that sort of influence?

Another question that also came up concerned the competition this would generate, which would effect another shop in the village that also sold alcoholic drinks. This question was put aside as not being the concern of the parish council. That was something that had to be worked out in the course of trade. Both these decisions showed a healthy understanding of the true task of the rights sector.

In every community of human beings there must be an organ, a group of people who are able to sense what is felt by the community, what arises as common opinion as to what is just and fair, what is right moral behavior between people, and to establish an ordering of community affairs accordingly.

The Earthly State

So we have the earthly state, the proper sphere of democracy. In this all people have to be seen and treated as equal. But equality in the state can only be achieved at the cost of the denial of individuality, of masking the uniqueness of each person. The policeman, the tax inspector, and the immigration officer are all servants of the state. To fulfil their role in society they have to apply the law equally to every person. They must refrain from seeing people as individuals. It is necessary that they are able to put aside, to be blind to the color, sex, or different abilities of people, and their ethnic origins. They must not, for example, apply the law in one way to people for whom they feel a sympathy, and in another way to those to whom they feel antipathy, or who are different from themselves.

This is not easy. It can be experienced as dehumanizing, both to the one who has to apply the law and the one to whom it must be applied. Anyone who has been caught up on the wrong side of the law will know this out of direct experience. This feeling of the inhumanity of the law is experienced by very many people and explains much of the antipathy felt towards the state or the government.

It is only the individual human being administering the law who can give it a human touch, a human face. But to do this he must know when to apply it and when not; he must go beyond the law.

It is important that every school or such institution consciously establish a body to be responsible for the rights life of the organization. This can be one that also has other responsibilities, but it must know when it is acting in the one sphere or the other. This will be looked at in more detail later in Chapter Thirteen.

But there is another "equality." If we look at the threefold human being of body, soul, and spirit, we see that to provide for the needs of the physical body we have to work out of mutuality, of brotherhood. In the sphere of the soul, in the cultural life of the community, we have to arrive at individual freedom. This is the sphere of individuality, of the blossoming of that which each person brings uniquely with them through birth from worlds of soul and spirit.

In his spirit every human being must be seen as equal. In this era of the consciousness soul humanity strives for the Spirit Self. This is something that is as yet no more than a potentiality in the earthly human being. In their aspirations towards this all people are equal. In every human being there is that which is "of the nature of the Divine." In the inner sanctuary, in the inner-most being of every person we meet over the whole earth, there is that which is "of God," which is universal. This is something that is equal in every human being, but which is not yet on the earth.

When we meet another person, we see their physical bodily form. And we see expressed through this something of the soul, its individual nature, its uniqueness. But in our time we do not see that which is of the spirit in the other. We only see what is different, not that which is universally human. If we did, we would not need the state, or the outer law. Then we would not be able to harm the other. To hurt the other would be hurting something that was also in ourselves. We would actually feel the pain of the other.

It is important that we distinguish between the earthly realm of the state and the realm of the Spirit which is "not of this earth."

Conscience and Law

There are times when there is conflict between, on the one side, the law and those whose task it is to uphold it, and on the other, those who are prompted to action by the voice of their conscience as to what is right and moral. This opposition lay behind such conflicts as the ban-the-bomb protests, the anti- road-building, and much of the kind of activity that Greenpeace in-volves itself with.

For example, if the majority of people in a community understand, or believe, that experiments on animals are necessary in the production of medicines needed to heal people and for the saving of lives, and they are also of the opinion that in those circumstances such experiments are justified and should be carried out, then within the rights life it is appropriate that this activity be made lawful. Those then carrying out the experiments are doing what is sanctioned by the law and supported by the common opinion of the majority. Their activity is within the law and must be protected from those who might want to hinder them. We are looking at this purely from the point of view as to whether the experiments should be allowed within the law. Whether public opinion is properly informed of the real facts is not for those working in rights life to decide. They must be guided only by what public opinion is.

But there may well be a number of people in that community who feel very strongly otherwise, and not for any reason of personal benefit. This opposition may come from a deep sense of what is moral and what is immoral. It may be so deeply felt that individuals are prepared to put themselves to considerable suffering to stand for what they see as right, as what is good and moral. Can we really say that they are wrong and must conform to the will of the majority? The law by its nature cannot be flexible. To make exceptions would require an authority outside rights life to judge who should be excepted. It would require capacities of discernment that have no place in rights life. That itself would negate much of the effectiveness and authority of the work of the rights life.

Is it not also commonly felt that a person is right to stand up for what he believes? Do not most people also sense that moral and social development takes place when people do have the courage of their convictions?

In this situation it is not possible to say that one side is right and the other wrong. In a certain sense both are right, but they are opposite. When we see this contrast between the implacable and dehumanizing nature of the written earthly law and that of the moral law, the law of our spiritual nature, something of the character of rights life is revealed.

Chapter Five

Economics - Division of Labor

I give you thanks, cold silent Stone,
And bend me down in awe before you.
From you the plant in me has grown.

I give you thanks, green Grass and Flower,
And stoop in reference before you.
You let me win the beast's swift power.

I thank you all, Plant, Beast, and Stone
And bow in gratitude before you.
You led, all three, to me alone.

We give thanks, bright Child and Star,
And kneel us down in love before you.
For because thou art, we are.

Thanks flow from all the Gods and Lands,
And from each God again expands.
In thanks all Being joins its hands.

The Washing of the Feet
– Christian Morgenstern

The term "economic," as it is generally used, can have wide and varied meanings. It is therefore, necessary, for the purpose of this study and for an understanding of the three spheres of social life, to come to a more precise meaning of the term.

In order to live, and before we can become involved in any inner life of soul, we must first be provided with the material necessities needed to live. We must have food and water, clothing, housing, heat, tools and utensils, and much else. Today, particularly in the developed world, what are considered essentials for a reasonable standard of living would include much more than just these basics, for example, a television set and a car.

In this study by the term "economic," I refer to all human activity involved in the production and distribution of the goods and services that fulfill these human needs. We can say that cultural life provides for the needs of the soul-spiritual nature and economic life for the needs of the physical body.

This should not be confused with the growth, earning, and accumulation of money. Today economic life is generally seen in terms of money, and the actual activity of producing the goods and services is lost sight of. Money arises out of this process of economic production. It facilitates and makes very much possible, but it itself is not the economy. It does not satisfy any of the needs of the body; it cannot be eaten, worn, or lived in. The movement and working of money is not itself economic activity. We will look further into the nature of money in Chapter Eight.

We must also distinguish between the economic sphere proper, that is the actual activity of production that produces the goods and services we need, and those things which are not products of the economic process and do not belong in that sphere, but which have come to be treated as economic products. Here I refer to such things as the sale and purchase of land, labor, shares, and education. Each of these is considered in more detail elsewhere in this book.

To come to see what is and what is not a true part of the economic process, of the economic sphere, is an essential foundation to an understanding of the threefold social order.

Another important point to bear in mind is the place from which we view economic life. We can view it from the place at which we each stand, or from the periphery, from the community as a whole. By this I mean that each can consider the economy subjectively, that is from the point of view of what is most advantageous for himself, or it can be viewed objectively from the point of view as to how it can work best for the benefit of all people, how can the whole economy work in such a way that sufficient is produced for everyone, and that everyone receives what they need. In this study we are looking at economic life from the point of view of the needs of the community as a whole, not from that of the individual. By "individual" I mean the individual person or individual organization. We are not considering personal or institutional economics. We take as our starting point the view that the task of the economic sphere of social life is to organize itself in such a way that it produces what is needed by the community as a whole and distributes to each member that which is needed by each one. The community here can only be the world community. The problems of the poor, the hungry, and the homeless will never be solved on the basis of each person looking after themselves.

Whenever we consider economics, we should be clear as to whether we are concerned with the economy of the individual – how do I earn enough and look after my economic needs? –

and the economy of the community as a whole. Quite different laws apply in each case, and much of the problems today arise due to the failure to make a proper distinction between these two. Very often what is seen as a beneficial way of working from the perspective of the individual is actually destructive for the whole.

A further point: If we look at the economic and cultural spheres, we will come to see that they are related to each other as are polar opposites. In nearly every aspect what is healthy for the one works adversely for the other. What works in one direction in the one works in the opposite direction in the other. For example, in economic life we are constantly led to humanity as a whole, to one world, to a world economy. In cultural life we come always to the single person, to the uniqueness and individuality of each human being.

The economic sphere is probably by far the most complex and difficult of the three to grasp. It requires powers of observation and imaginative picture thinking beyond what most people are used to. Here we can only try to grasp something of its basic nature. What is important is not that one fully understands it (that actually is not possible), but that one develops a sense for it, a feeling for its nature. Then we can see how it relates to the school or other cultural institution.

The Start of the Economic Process

Let us look at something of the economic productive process. All economic products have their origin in nature or subnature. We can trace everything we use, wear, eat, or in any other way consume, to its origin in nature. The actual economic process starts when human labor takes hold of the products of nature and transforms them. This can be by working on the substance and changing it, as when wood is made into a table, or by merely moving it to the place where it is to be used, as when the finished table is moved from the factory to the shop, or coal from in the earth to the fire place.

Human intelligence or ingenuity makes human labor more efficient or productive. It does this through what we term "division-of-labor." This can take two forms but is usually a combination of both. Either the work to be done is divided between a number of people, so that each concentrates on one part of the productive process, or it enables some people to make "tools" which in themselves are not needed, but which enable others to work more productively in producing what is needed. Division-of-labor consists in the interplay between two factors, human labor working on nature on the one side, and on the other, the human creative capacity making the human labor more efficient and productive.

Division-of-Labor

Division-of-labor lies at the foundation of economic life; it gives to it its particular nature and laws. It can be shown, in its very simplest form, by an imaginative picture.

Because economic life is so complex and difficult to observe, it is often necessary to consider it in its simplest state, where the many other factors at play are reduced to a minimum. In this way we can see what is also at work in the most complex economic productive processes but which is hidden there. Imagine a very simple community (one such that probably never existed) where every one makes whatever they need for themselves. There is no division-of-labor, no sharing of the work.

"A" decides to make himself a shirt. He also needs a pot. We can easily see that each of these will involve considerable work, from the gathering up of the materials and the making of any necessary tools to the actual making of the shirt and the pot.

Now suppose there is another person, "B," who also needs to make a shirt and a pot. He also will have to do the same amount of work. What happens if one of them gets the idea and suggests that "A," in making a shirt for himself, instead of then making a pot, makes a second shirt for "B." In the same way "B" will not make a shirt for himself but will make a second pot for "A."

Now the whole situation is changed. "A" makes a shirt for himself. At the same time he also makes one for "B." We can see that the first shirt that he makes for himself will still take the same amount of activity as before, but the second will take considerably less. So in making a second shirt there is a bonus. It is made with less time and effort than it would have taken if "B" had made it, or we could say that the work becomes more productive. The same applies to the making of the second pot by "B" for "A."

What is apparent here is the principle that when the work is divided, when a person makes a thing also for another person, it becomes more productive. This principle is the foundation of all economic production, from the simple situation of a person using a spade to dig the ground for the growing of vegetables to the most complex industrial processes, such as the manufacture of motor cars or the computer. It is what makes it possible for each of us to acquire products that it would be impossible for us to have if we had to make them for ourselves. For example, if I had to make an electric light bulb on my own, including the gathering up of the raw materials, it would take me years. But because of division-of-labor, I can buy one with the money that it takes the average person to earn in a matter of minutes.

"A" and "B" then exchange the shirt for the pot. In this way "A" gets his pot, not by making a pot with all that that entails, but by the much simpler means of making a second shirt for "B." Each in making something, not for himself but for the other, gets what he wants but with less effort, and so is better off. The difference in the value between what each makes and gives to the other, and the value of what each receives is "profit." This profit is always there in economic life. It is that which keeps it in movement. Without it there would be no economic life as we know it.

Purchase and Sale

The exchange, or purchase, brings back together that which was first separated out. It is the completion of a process, not a totality in itself. A true purchase is one that is the completion of a process that starts with the separating out in division-of-labor. With the complexity of economic life today, when money comes into the transaction, it is almost impossible to see this, but this element of the completion of a process is nevertheless always there. That which is divided out in division-of-labor is reinstated in sale and purchase, so that each then receives that which he needs.

In the sale and purchase "A" receives the pot which was what he wanted in the first place, but which he himself did not make because the work was divided - he made a second shirt.

In this over simplified picture we see all the fundamental factors of division-of-labor, factors that are the foundation for the whole of our economic process of production and distribution. We see human labor that is organized and made more productive by thinking, by the imaginative, inventive capacity.

Here we see it in its very simplest form, but it is there also in the most complex of industrial production processes.

Altruism and Mutuality

In division-of-labor we can see that basic to the increased productive efficiency that arises is the fact that each person must move from making for himself the things he himself needs to making for other people what they need. When we say that in economic production we must work out of altruism, out of brotherhood, we are not speaking from a basis of ethics or morality. In economic life we will not achieve anything that way. We mean nothing more than is shown here, that when in the sphere of economic activity we put aside our own needs and work to produce what others need, then economic activity becomes more productive, then we all have more. This is a fundamental law of the economic sphere of activity and should be taken into account at all levels of community economic life. With regard to the economic aspects of an organization, which in this would include money, the less each part or department is able to act and make decisions out of its own interests and the more decisions are made in relationship to the whole, the better off all will be.

When I look at all I have and will own, use, or consume through my life, there is no way I could produce even a thousandth part of it for myself if I worked alone, no matter how skilled I was and how hard I worked.

This "mutuality" is what gives to economic life its particular character and orientation. It will be gone into in more detail in the next chapter.

The Woodcutters, the Place of Capital

And now we can look at division-of-labor as it evolves further with another imaginative picture. Imagine a simple village community, surrounded by forest, and of necessity the people having to provide for themselves as a community. They need wood for cooking and for keeping warm. There are ten woodcutters, who all work independently of each other. Each goes out to his particular part of the forest and cuts the wood. Each then brings the day's product back to market and there sells it. Let us say that each cuts 10 units of wood per day. (Too much importance should not be attached to the actual figures; they are only there to help perceive change, to see the process of the creating of value and its accumulation.) So 100 units of wood come each day to the community. We will assume that this does not really meet their needs.

Now imagine that one of the woodcutters has an idea. He decides that he will not cut any more wood. He will get a horse and cart and each day will collect what the others have cut, and he will take it to market to sell. The now 9 woodcutters do not have to transport their wood, nor sit in the market selling it. That means they can concentrate on cutting wood. Without taking any more time or doing any more work than they did before, they now produce more wood, say 13 units each. So 117 units of wood now come to the community, and they are better off. The man with the cart, the Carter, charges two units to each of the woodcutters, so he earns 18 units, and the woodcutters are left with 11 units each. Everyone is better off than before. Here we see the dividing of the labor. The woodcutters are now divided into those who cut the wood and the one who moves and sells it in the market. So more is produced and comes to the community, although no one works any harder.

We could, of course, question why the Carter is so much better off than the others. This is a critical question of our time that must be dealt with. But it is one that cannot be considered within the scope of this book. For the moment we are looking at the economic process, at what actually happens, not at what ought to happen, or is morally justified. What is important to see here is that profit does arise and that somewhere within the community this can be accumulated as capital.

We have used the term "units" of wood. We could say "units of value." The economic value of the wood can be represented either by the wood itself or by money. The wood could be used as a means of exchange and so itself become money.

The Carter spends 12 units of value a day on himself. He lives at a slightly higher level of expenditure than the others, and he stores 6. In this way he accumulates units of value, or money. This stored money takes on a quite different nature from that money which is spent daily; it has a different "value." It has the potential of releasing human creativity, of human soul capacities. It becomes "capital."

Now the next stage of the development of the economic process: Imagine that one of the nine woodcutters comes up with an idea, an idea of a tool that will make the cutting of wood much more effective. More wood could be cut with the same labor and time, or the same wood with less labor and time. But as an idea in his head, it will not cut wood. Economically, it is quite useless, so long as it remains in the realm of idea. It must be brought down into material substance; only then can it cut wood. What must first be there to make this possible? Capital must be available to the person with the idea. Only then can he create the workshop, or smithy, in which to make the tools.

We can also ask how did the Carter obtain his cart and horse? How did he obtain his capital? The potential for that must have been somewhere present. The thinking, creative capacity in the human being, working into economic activity will create capital. It is capital that releases, makes possible the creative genius to work into, to fructify the economic process.

The man with the idea (we will call him the Smith), will borrow the capital from the Carter. With this he will set up his smithy and start bringing his idea into substance, into actual tools. Now that which happened when the Carter started working with his cart also happens as a result of the tools, the wood saws, of the Smith. There will be only 8 woodcutters cutting wood, but using the new saws they will cut even more than before, so more wood will be coming to market for the community. The Smith will himself also start accumulating capital. He repays the Carter.

The Nature of Capital

The money that the Carter lent to the Smith has taken on a different nature and function from that which it had when it came into being as purchase money. Its value is not the same as it was as purchase money. (We are, of course, considering this from the point of view of the community as a whole, not from the interests of any one individual or group of people.) Then its value was the same as that for which it was exchanged. The value is now related to the potential of the idea of the person to whom it is lent. If his idea is impractical, then the capital lent to him will have little or no value; it will be wasted. But in practice it is the productive ideas that attract loans and give the capital a value; the loan increases the productivity of the woodcutters. It brings about an increase.

Now we can say that the money as capital lent to the person with the fruitful idea has a greater value than it had as purchase money. As purchase money it enabled the economic process to continue on its normal course. As loan or investment capital, it enables an increase, a development, which will continue to benefit into the future. Money does not have a value that is the same wherever it is in the economic process. The value of $2,000 is different when it is in the realm of sale and purchase or as loan capital. Again it is different if, as loan or investment capital, it is placed in the hands of an entrepreneur, an ordinary consumer, or a playboy. We need to remember that we are, of course, basing our considerations on the interests of the community as a whole.

The question can now be asked, what is the nature of the capital that the Carter passed to the Smith? Is it correct to treat this as a loan? If we look at the economic process, we see that this money capital, taken hold of by the idea of the Smith, results in the capital reproducing itself. The original capital was used up, but through the use of the tools created by the Smith, more capital is now generated. Within the economic process money passed to and used by human ingenuity recreates itself; the economic process itself repays the capital. Due to this fact it can only be a loan. Even if the Carter gives the money to the Smith the economic process reproduces it, repays it. It is, therefore, loan capital. It is for this reason that we tend to use the term "loan" rather than "investment."

We can also now see that it is a necessity for the development of the economic process that capital be accumulated. If the Carter had spent all his money, or if the increase had been evenly distributed between the Carter and the woodcutters, and so probably spent, the Smith could not have made his idea fruitful, and the community would not have had the benefit of the increased productivity. It must be possible for money, profit, to accumulate somewhere. Whether this should be in the hands of the Carter, or the Smith, or some other body is not a question within the scope of this book. For the present it need only be recognized that the creation of capital is a necessary part of economic life.

This process will, of course, continue. Another woodcutter will come up with an idea, borrow capital, and make the labor of cutting wood more productive. This can repeat itself until a time comes when too much wood is produced, and too much capital accumulates. In addition, too many trees will be cut down. Division-of-labor, which at first benefits humanity, when allowed to develop uncontrolled, will come to work destructively. We see this often – something that starts out as of benefit to humanity, if allowed to develop unchecked, without human conscious control, grows beyond its beneficial origin and becomes harmful. We see this factor at work in almost all our financial institutions.

An excess of capital comes about when there is more than is needed for the healthy development or maintenance of the economic process.

As we saw, the more human thinking enters into the economic process, the more efficient and productive the process becomes, and the more humanity is freed from labor. But the labor that is still done becomes dead, and it loses all that quality of soul nourishment that working directly with nature or at the crafts gives. To see this, we only have to look at the labor involved in the economic processes that gives us the motor car or television at prices that enable all to have them.

There is a limit to the capital that can be used up in this way. When more capital is generated, the capital that cannot be so used up beneficially within economic life will then develop something of a cancerous nature within the social fabric. It will try to preserve itself, try to grow, to increase its value. It achieves this in different ways, but particularly in the creation of capital values in areas outside the economic process, that is by assigning economic value to "rights." This can be seen, for instance, in rising land prices, and in the huge sums of money caught up in stocks and shares, in the money markets and in foreign exchange dealings, and in the purchase of works of art with the resulting exorbitantly high monetary values. This is one of the major questions of today, how to deal with the tendency to generate too much capital, too much accumulated money.

How can the harmful effects of division-of-labor be counteracted? How can the excess capital be used up instead of being allowed to accumulate in a way that becomes harmful to the social fabric, and how can the economic process be controlled in such a way that only as many products as are needed are actually produced and the nature resources are not wasted? These are the questions of today, questions that can only be answered through a healthy and challenging cultural life based on a knowledge of the spirit that works through all of life.

Work and the Consequences of Division-of-Labor

When division-of-labor spreads beyond the two "A" and "B," to the whole community, the exchange becomes very much more complicated. That which "A" wants may be produced by "B," but what "B" wants produced by "C." At this point money must enter the scene to facilitate exchange. As it grows ever more complex, the true nature of production through division-of-labor and exchange becomes hidden and lost sight of. I no longer see that when I buy a product I am completing a process that started when the work of producing it was divided and in which many thousands of people and processes may have been involved.

I am able to acquire an electric light bulb for a small fraction of what I earn, for the equivalent of a few minutes work. But the people who work on the economic process based on division-of-labor, which makes this possible, must do work that itself no longer satisfies anything of their own inner soul needs. In the evolving of division-of-labor, all that which, in the labor, formerly nourished the human soul has been squeezed out. It is not possible to have both: the highly productive work and the soul nourishment. Of course, the example of the manufacture of the electric light bulb is an extreme. In most work there is a varying degree of inner fulfillment. But the more division-of-labor enters into the activity, the less human fulfillment will be experienced. The work that an artist, a teacher, or a research scientist does, if he is any good at his work, will in almost all cases be an outcome of impulses and needs that lie within his own soul. In his work he will find a satisfying of these needs. The person who works at the machine producing some small part for many electric light bulbs does not do so out of any such inner need. He produces bulbs, because the humanity of our time needs them.

We must be clear as to the nature of economic work. A polarity was described earlier in Chapter Three between the two types of work: between the work that is done because it fulfills something in the one who does the work, and that which is done because it fulfills a need of others, not the one doing the work. This was there pointed to as the polarity that exists between work in the cultural sphere and that in the economic sphere. Of course, there is always something of both poles in all work, but in each sphere the work is mostly at one pole or the other.

This polarity between the cultural and economic spheres is also to be found within the economic sphere itself. Most work in economic life is near that pole where there is nothing or little that nourishes the life of the soul. At or near this pole are those who work at the machine in the factory, or as a bricklayer, laborer, shop salesperson, or cashier. But the work of the entrepreneur or the manager of a business is nearer to the opposite pole. It is in this work that the individual impulses and capacities that arise in the soul find expression. The manager is really a half free cultural worker. It is the person in the factory who is the true economic worker.

It is this pole, this half free cultural work within the economic sphere, that has achieved the enormous developments in products and economic production of recent times. What I have referred to as division-of-labor for purposes of clarity would include what we now call technology. This half free cultural life, half free because here human creativity and imagination are bound within the needs and laws of the economic sphere, is actually more exciting and appealing to the soul for many people than most of our cultural life proper.

"Purchase" of Labor

It is a widespread assumption that labor can be and is purchased. But if we follow through the process of division-of-labor, we will see that it is always the product of labor that has value, that is exchanged or purchased. The labor itself, as labor, has no economic value. It creates a value, but that value is in the product. We eat, wear, or otherwise use the products of labor, not the labor. That itself is of no use except to produce a product which is what is wanted and is of use.

Imagine a person working in a factory producing engines, for example, on a conveyor belt system. A partially completed engine comes before him, and he does a certain amount of work on it before it moves on to the next worker. We can ask what it is he is paid for. Does management purchase the movements he makes, the energy he expends? Or do they purchase the product, the change that resulted from his work that brought the engine that much nearer to completion?

At the end of the line the engine is complete. It can be put in a car, and it will propel it forward. It is the completed engine, the sum total of all the changes that took place that is sold and put in the car and that moves it, not the accumulated movements, etc., of the workers.

There is an enormous difference in thinking in terms of purchasing a person's labor, or the product of his labor. Not only is it economically untrue, but a person feels that he is selling something of himself when he experiences his labor as being purchased. His individuality is violated. This has social consequences. The question of salaries or wages is looked at from several aspects later in the book.

Chapter Six

Economics –
Mutuality and Associations

Egoism and Mutuality

In contrast to cultural life, in the sphere of economic production, distribution, and consumption, we are all dependent on the whole community for the things that we need to live, work, and play. No individual can stand alone; no one can be self sufficient. We only need to observe all that we have and consume through life to know that there is no way in which we could, each by himself, produce more than a small fraction of what we use. It becomes clear, when we look closely at the working of economic activity, that in this realm of social life "mutuality" or "brotherhood" is called for by the process of production itself.

This mutuality or community gives to economic life its particular nature and differentiates it from the other two spheres of social life. The more we observe the sphere of economics, the more we come to see that we are always led away from the individual and to the group, to people working together, to humanity as a whole. The individual as individual can achieve virtually nothing.

People often talk about living on their salary or pension, or of being self sufficient. But this way of thinking is based on a widely held fallacy, that is, that we live on the money we have or earn. But we do not; we live on the products that other people work to produce. The money only gives us the power to acquire them. It does not produce them.

The individual who is thus dependent on mutuality within the community for the actual production of what he needs will nevertheless, in the first place, view the community from the perspective of his own needs, not the needs of the community. This cannot be otherwise.

We live in the age of the consciousness soul, of the awakening to a consciousness of self, of our "I," of our own individuality. But alongside this has come the birth of the industrial age, an economic life based on the development of division-of-labor, of interdependence. Just when within economics there is the greatest need to arrive at a conscious working for the community, human beings have arrived in their evolution at the point where they have to awaken to themselves as individuals, as opposed to being members of a group.

So, we come to a conflict that is deeply rooted in our time. We have seen that modern economic life, based as it is on division-of-labor, out of its own nature calls for mutuality. But it is the ingenuity and creativity kindled by egoism and nurtured in cultural life that sustains and enhances division-of- labor, that from which egoism must be excluded. And it is just those who are impelled by their own egoism to develop powers of imagi-nation, creativity, and entrepreneurial enterprise who are the managers and leaders of economic life, from which egoism needs to be excluded.

The individual human being will always approach eco-nomic life out of egoism. When we buy or sell, when we start or run a business, we think and act out of what is best for our-selves. This is also true of the individual organization, whether it is a school or a manufacturing enterprise.

Center and Periphery

We each look after our own needs by observing and act-ing from the place where we individually stand. From the point of view of the individual person or institution, this is necessary. But we cannot in this way come to an understanding of the work-ing of the economic life of the community as a whole and how it can provide for all within the community.

It makes a very great difference to our understanding and control of the community economic life if we act from the interests that arise at the point at which we individually stand, or if we act out of an interest in the needs of the whole commu-nity, that is, from the periphery. We can act out of the sense that we each have to struggle to make a living, each for himself within the community of human beings, where all others also act out of self interest, that each is a separate center within the economy. Or we can see the task of the economic sector as a whole as be-ing responsible for producing everything that is needed by the community as a whole. In the end that means for all humanity. Both viewpoints are valid within their own fields, but it makes an enormous difference to the social life of the community, if we fail to find a form which gives the necessary guidance and control to the needs of the whole. Due to modern technological developments today humanity has the ability to provide for every human being on this earth. That there are so many who are not provided for is not because we cannot provide for them, but because we have not the thoughts with which to take hold of economic life and structure it in such a way that the whole is provided for. In cultural life we start from the impulses and needs of the individual. In economic life we must start from the needs and interests of the whole. The major question now is: How do we form the economic life so that we can bring about this control from the periphery?

This cannot be achieved by rules and regulations issued from the rights sphere, by government. No legislation or outer authority, such as the law, will ever get people of themselves to think and act out of mutuality, to act out of brotherhood or sisterhood. If they do not do that, then they will devote their energies to finding ways around the law.

The organ of the rights sphere, the government, has to establish the boundaries within which economic life must be free to work. These boundaries will include the access to natural resources and its effect on the environment, and the actual conditions of employment of those who work in the economic sphere. But as we saw, the nature of rights life is always arbitrary and inflexible. It only has a necessary purpose when people cannot of themselves act in a social way. If those who work in economic life were themselves able to put aside their own egoistic needs and interests, it would not be necessary to have the laws to keep them within certain bounds. But though the law can prevent people from acting antisocial in certain areas, it cannot make them act socially in others. For this something else must be found.

Unsolvable Problems of Today

Let us look at some of the problems of our time, problems that seem to be getting worse but which seem impossible to overcome, despite the best efforts of many sincere and well meaning people in both industry and in government. One such problem is unemployment. Another, closely related, is the growing divide between the well paid and the poorly paid, the rich and the poor. These are two of the problems that cannot be solved by the individual, that is the single person, organization, or business. There are many more such problems, particularly connected to the environment and to health.

The individual businessman or entrepreneur cannot by himself deal with these problems, no matter how much we may think that he morally ought to. Imagine a situation where a person sets up a business making furniture. If he is to be successful, he must give all his attention to his business; he must want to produce good furniture, better than that of other furniture makers. He will want people to buy his products, and he will want to make a profit. He must be interested in the enhancing of his own business and the improvement of his products. He will naturally approach his work with a certain egoism. Of course, all furniture makers will act in the same way. The aim to produce a better product than others is a healthy form of competition and one that benefits the community. To think that people ought to act otherwise is to fail to understand the nature of human evolution and the needs of our time.

If he is successful, his business will expand, and he will, among other things, take on more employees. But then a time might come when his business contracts. This can be for any number of reasons and might be beyond his control. It could be that there is a general recession, and people are just not buying furniture. He cannot just ignore this, but he must reduce his costs in order to save his business. Quite clearly he cannot go on paying out the same amount of money when the income is greatly reduced. He might do many things to alleviate the situation, but eventually he will have to get rid of some of his employees. They will become unemployed. It is often the case that there will be other businesses also laying off their workers, so that there is an increase in unemployment.

Clearly the individual businesses acting independently cannot solve this question, not even if just a few of them get together. They can only act in isolation within their own narrow sphere. But such problems arise out of the working of the whole economy. Only the economy as a whole is self contained; the individual business never is. The individual business can solve its problems by getting rid of workers, who are then outside and no longer its concern. But they become the concern of the community, of the whole, and they can never be outside that.

The polarity between the individual and the whole community is one of great importance and needs to be fully recognized, if we are to find a solution to these problems. The individual enterprise can deal with problems in so far as they relate to that enterprise. It cannot solve the problems of the whole community. For that there must be some organ that has a consciousness and sense of the needs of the whole.

Associative Working Together

It is possible to form such an organ. Rudolf Steiner spoke of what in English is referred to as "economic associations," or as working "associatively." This use of the word "association" should not be confused with the general concept today of an "association" as a group of people or organizations with like interest, who associate to protect or enhance their own interests, sometimes at a cost to others. On the contrary, this is where individuals work together in order to reach beyond the interests of the individuals to that of the whole.

The forming of such associations is based on a phenomenon that can be observed and the nature of which needs to be fully recognized and understood.

The individual entrepreneur must, in the first place, concern himself with the running and development of his own enterprise. He has to work out of a form of egoism in so far as the interests of his enterprise are concerned. As was seen above, it is to the advantage of the community that he do so.

When the individual entrepreneurs, producers, traders and consumers come together to work associatively, each from their particular place in the economic sphere of activity, then it is possible for something to be born in the group that cannot be achieved by the individual alone. Each individual brings with him an understanding of the economy that is gained from his particular position in it. The baker will see the economy from a different perspective from that of the farmer, who again will see it differently from that of the shopkeeper. The relationship of the baker to the farmer is that of a consumer, but to the shopkeeper he is a supplier. Not only will they see it differently, they will each act out of the egoism of their particular place in the economy as a whole. The individual can do no other. The belief that the individual working in economic life can see the whole objectively and can act out of the interest of the whole, out of mutuality or brotherhood, arises out of a failure to grasp the nature of economic life.

But when these individuals come together in the right way, then the group can rise above the egoism of the individual. "The objective community spirit" can arise within the group. The group can develop an imagination of the whole that the individual alone cannot do; it can become more than the sum total of the individual members. If the members come together in the right mood of soul, then the imagination of the whole community emerges as though living in the center of those who come together.

If people would observe life more carefully, they would be aware of this, that when people come together and carry into their meeting a will to work for the whole, then the group can rise above the egoism of the individual members and become aware of the community as a whole. It often happens. But it passes unnoticed and so has not been taken hold of.

I personally have experienced this. On one particular occasion I was involved in a meeting where a number of people came together to solve a particular problem. They were all involved in different but connected areas in a line of production, distribution, and consumption. I personally knew most of the people involved, and had experienced in each their particular egoism, their wanting to gain any benefit for their own particular enterprise. But it was a remarkable experience to see how they changed when they came together. It was as though a common imagination of the totality of their work, of the whole community, touched each one, and they spoke and acted out of that total imagination.

This transformation, or presence, that comes into a group when people come together in the right mood of soul is of immense importance. It is the only organ that can, firstly, develop a true imagination of the economy as a totality, and secondly, kindle the will in the individual to act out of the interests of the whole.

True associative working can have no boundaries, no division between those within and those without. Even when an association is concerned with one narrow line of production, its "objective community spirit" must reach to the whole of humanity. Although its immediate concern may be narrow, it is, nevertheless, a part of and ultimately concerned with the whole.

Members of the association need to be drawn from those who have expert knowledge and who represent areas of economic life within the whole spectrum of production, distribution, and consumption and should include representatives from management and manual workers. They must be able to come together, not as representatives to concern themselves with the interests of those whom they represent, but because they each stand and have knowledge in a different field of the economy and have come to recognize that all individuals benefit only when the interests of the whole are put first. The alternative is that the few can benefit at the cost of the majority. That this is the situation today is plainly visible for all to see.

It is also a reality that a person whose main work is in cultural life, where egoism has a rightful place, will have great difficulty in working fruitfully in an association. A person whose work lies in economic activity, where mutuality is at the core of the activity, will have much greater ability to arrive at an objective imagination of the whole.

The association, or associative way of working, is the proper form of management of economic life. It would not be the right way for the cultural or rights spheres.

Chapter Seven

Cultural/Economic
The Two Poles

We need now to pull a number of threads together to form a more complete picture of the reciprocal interweaving between the economic and cultural spheres. To do this I will first bring together some of the polarities we have already touched on.

The Single Individual / The Whole Community

The economic sphere of social life becomes efficient only when it finds its purpose in the requirements of the whole community, when it is directed from the periphery. There the individual human being can achieve nothing by himself. Only when he works in association with others does his work become effective. Economic activity concerns itself with the substances and forces of earthly material life.

In cultural life it is the single person that is important, that must be the focus of attention. Only the individual human being can come to a truth, an artistic creation. A group cannot do this. The group can achieve this only to the extent that each individual within the group does so. In cultural life we have to concern ourselves with the supersensible nature of the human being. There the individual has to find his way for himself.

In so far as a person works truly in economic life, that is, in the actual activity of production - "on the factory floor," not in management - he is working, not out of his own needs or resolves, but out of the needs of humanity, out of world karma. A person working at the machine involved in the production of electric light bulbs does so because human beings, at this time of human evolution, need electric light.

In cultural life a person works primarily out of his own karma, out of those intentions and capacities that he brought with him from his time before birth. He must first work to develop his own capacities and a knowledge of himself.

In cultural life the individual must follow that ancient call "Man know thyself." In economic life the individual has to forget himself, has to "awaken to the community, to humanity."

Social life must strive to bring balance between these two poles, between that which is striven for out of the need for self expression, out of egoism, and that which is done, not for one's own benefit but for that of humanity, out of altruism. This should become a rhythm within social life, a breathing in and a breathing out.

In Cultural Life - No Division of Labor, No Economic Exchange

In economic life a purchase, which involves an exchange, is the completion, the bringing together that which was first separated out in division-of-labor. In cultural life there is no "division-of-labor," so there can be no similar exchange. Payment can only be something like a contribution, which frees the individual capacities for work into the future.

This might appear idealistic, or unreal. But it is, nevertheless, what actually happens. Anyone who really observes both the economic and cultural spheres of activity, and is able to put aside the prevailing ways of thinking which derive from economic life, will see this.

Some people do think that the specialization of subjects in a school - that one teaches painting, another language, another science, is a form of division-of-labor. But it is not so; it is entirely different. The one who teaches painting does not divide the work out in the same way. He specializes in the one subject in order to deepen his understanding of it, to develop his skills and to grasp the underlying nature, the spiritual foundation, of the subject. The possibility to specialize leads to a certain enrichment. In economic life division-of-labor leads in the opposite direction. The person caught up in it will know less and less of what he is involved in, will feel separated from the products of his work, and will find very little or even nothing in his work to satisfy the needs of his life of soul.

Economic/Cultural - The Balancing of Gifts

We have seen how in the economic sector when the capacities of imagination and invention are brought to bear on the productive process, on the one side the process is made more productive (more commodities are produced), and on the other side more capital is generated. If this increase is not used up, it will of necessity accumulate, and the accumulations will work against the well-being of society. The human spirit within economic life has the urge always to invent, to create new technologies, to find new ways of making a profit. The economic life of itself will invariably have the tendency to become more efficient, to produce more, to create surpluses.

We see this, on the one side in the huge accumulations of capital that move through the foreign exchanges, futures, and other financial markets and the stock exchanges, as well as the increasing land values. On the other side, we see the constant pressure for people to buy and use more products. The enormous development and spread of and pressure for people to buy and use "information technology" is an example of this.

If these surpluses are not to continue to accumulate into something akin to cancerous growths in the social organism, there must be something there alongside the economic life which uses them up, something that is, so far as economic life is concerned, a pure consumer.

Industrial activity is made increasingly more productive by the imaginative, inventive capacity of the human being, by that which arises in a healthy living cultural life. In the example of the woodcutters, it was the imagination of the Carter and then the Smith which caused an increase in the production of wood, and in the accumulation of capital. The inventor is able to invent, because he lives in a society where the cultural life is one in which the creative capacities are nurtured. But there can be a free cultural life of the community only so long as those who create and nourish it are provided with the products of economic life, which they need in order to live and to do their work.

From the point of view of economic production, or industry, those who work in cultural life are, economically, pure consumers. As we have seen, the teacher, the musician, the poet, the athlete, and the entertainer do not produce economic products, but they do consume them. This also applies to those who work in the rights sphere. Economically, they, too, are pure consumers. They are actually necessary to economic life. As such, they balance the tendency to continued increased productivity. If they were not there, if instead they worked in economic life, even more would be produced. The problem would become worse, not easier.

We saw in the example of the lecturer that the money he received was not the result of a purchase, but was a gift or contribution. Those whose work lies in the cultural sphere can do so only if they receive what cannot be described otherwise.

In fact, the only way to prevent the excess capital accumulating within economic life, which if held there grows into something which can be seen as a cancerous growth within the social fabric, is by finding a way of passing it over to cultural life. With this money those who work in cultural life purchase what would otherwise be the excess production of economic life.

What is being described here is what in an arbitrary way actually does happen when the state taxes businesses and individuals and then passes the money to cultural life, to schools, etc. A tax is a form of compulsory gift; something is taken without anything being given directly in return. The question must be asked as to whether this is the best and most efficient way to remove the excess accumulations of capital from the sphere of economic activity. Are those whose work lies in the sphere of "rights," of that area where every person's opinion is of equal value, the best people to decide from where in economic life money should be taken, and to where in cultural life it should be given? And is sufficient money reaching cultural life to provide for the needs of the soul of every person in the community?

On the one side we have the economic sector producing what is needed by the community out of the substance of nature. It receives from the cultural sector that which fructifies it, increases its efficiency, makes it more productive. Due to this it produces surplus capital and surplus commodities.

On the other side we have the cultural sector nurturing the life of soul within the community. It needs the products of the economic sector in order to exist and fulfill its task. It brings into being those creative capacities which pass over into the economic sector.

Just as economic life must receive the renewing forces and the imaginative capacities from cultural life, so cultural life must receive the products from economic life. To achieve this, economic life must pass to cultural life the excess capital it creates, so that cultural life can buy those products it needs from economic life and so pass back, not capital, but the capital transformed back into purchase money. Let us look at two examples, two pictures:

Cultural Life: Consider money that is given to an institution of the cultural sphere. Such money will always be of the nature of capital. In a healthy social life it will have arisen as accumulated capital in economic life. When cultural life so often has to be supported out of income, it is a sign that the cultural and economic spheres are not in balance and working properly.

A donation of capital that is given to such an institution can be spent in two ways. For example, it may be paid as salaries for the cultural workers, such as the teachers, or it may be used to put up a new building, in which case it still ends up paying for the wages of the workers, or of those that provide the building materials. In both cases it ends up being used to buy the products needed for personal everyday life.

The capital as capital disappears. It dies into the new building and is reborn as purchase money, which passes back to economic life. The building itself, being for the purpose of cultural work, cannot be called capital in the economic sense.

Economic Life: Consider, for example, a crane. We see it lifting a heavy load to the place where it is needed. We can ask the question: "What is it that is lifting and moving that heavy weight, that is helping to put up that new building?"

We may, of course, say it is the crane, or that it is the engine in the crane, or that it is the combustion of the fuel that generates the power that actually does the lifting. We cannot say that any one answer is untrue; they are all in a certain way true. And yet do they really give the complete answer? What had to be there before any of them? The crane did not come together out of its own necessity; it did not create and assemble itself.

If we look at any part of the crane, whether it is a strut that forms part of the tower, or the steel cable that carries the strain of the lifting, or the pulley assembly round which the cable turns, or the parts of the engine, there we see human thought, human creativity. At every point we can see human thinking caught up into substance, into iron and steel. We can say that it is in reality human thought that lifts the load. But to do so, this thought had to die into substance. Once each part is made, the thought is no longer creative; it is dead. If thinking remained alive and active in the cran, then perhaps the crane could develop itself.

The crane is a tool; it is not an end product. It itself is not what we need, but it helps to produce that which we do need.

The thoughts themselves could not lift the load They had to be incorporated into physical form and substance. Just as we can see that capital comes into being in the economic realm and dies into cultural life – economically it disappears – so we can see that human thinking, creativity, nurtured in the cultural realm, dies into economic life. We are, of course, speaking only of that portion of human creativity that goes to nourishing economic activity.

We can show this by way of a diagram:

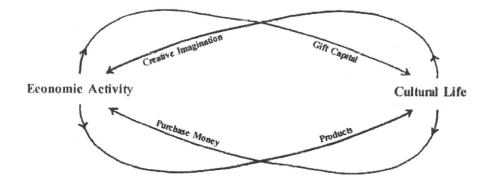

So, looking at human social life we see that which is nurtured in cultural life, which is there born and comes into being, passes over into economic life and there, united with loan capital, dies into substance, into machines and equipment. This in turn works towards the freeing of the individual human being from a life confined to labor and to the economic sphere.

In economic life we see that which comes into being as purchase money, evolving into capital, first as loan capital, and then as gift capital. It passes over to cultural life, and there as capital it dies. In dying it gives life and freedom to the awakening of the supersensible in the human being.

Chapter Eight

Money

Money gives the possibility of both good and evil. In its true reality it arises out of the economic process of production and distribution of products, when this activity is fructified by human imagination and creativity.

So long as it is bound and held in check by the true and separate working of the life of rights, and is enabled to die into and fructify the cultural life (that is, the sphere of activity of the human soul and spirit), it will work for good. But when it can run wild, unchecked, it will lead the human being to greed, power seeking, and the urge for self interest.

Although money is not itself one of the three spheres of social life, it plays an increasingly powerful role in our society and reaches far beyond the economic sphere out of which it arose. It has become something of far greater influence and power in our lives than we generally realize or acknowledge. It permeates all three spheres of social life, often in a way that brings great suffering and harm, and without grasping something of the nature of money and finance, it is not possible today to come to an understanding of the threefold nature of society.

Nor is money itself the economic sphere; it is closely connected to it but reaches beyond it. It is the productive process, the labor of many people that feeds, clothes, houses, and provides all our economical necessities, not the money. Money arises out of the combined working of the human creative spirit with human labor. It facilitates the economic process of production and distribution, but it itself is not the productive process.

Today we tend more and more to see money as a value in itself. We think in terms of living on an income or on a pension, that we have something because we paid for it; we stop there and do not see that we have it, because other people have labored to produce it. We do not think of what lies behind the money, what gives it value, what it represents. After all, we cannot eat it, wear it, nor does it keep us warm. It does nothing for us. Alone on a desert island I could have as much money as I liked, and it would be useless. Unless there are other people there producing the things that I need, the money can serve no purpose.

Money always represents, or stands for, a value of some kind, but is not itself the value. Its quality and nature vary as to where within the economic cycle it appears, and indeed whether it represents an economic value or some other kind of apparent value. From the point of view of the individual, it may seem unimportant how the money was acquired; the reality is what it will buy. But if we are in any way concerned for the well-being of society as a whole, it is immensely important that these things are taken into consciousness.

A school does not exist in isolation from the world. While it may be possible to achieve this within the cultural life, it is quite impossible to do so economically. The school and all the teachers and other staff live on the products produced by the economic activity of many thousands or millions of people. They could not teach, if there were not others working to produce what they need, and often doing work that does not provide the soul nourishment that teaching does or should do. On the level of the spirit, it is not enough to think that this dependence is resolved by paying money.

If those responsible for a school wish to manage money in a way that conforms with what is revealed by spiritual science, then it is necessary to first come to understand something of the economic process. Only then will they be able to work with money according to the true nature and the differing values of money, and with the spirit that works through the money.

Money is one of the most powerful and all embracing forces at work in the world in our time. With very few exceptions it touches every human being. It has a more universal control over people's actions and ways of life than probably anything else. But we are to a great extent unconscious of this influence that it has over us, which makes it so difficult to deal with. It is there in the language we use and in our ways of thinking and in our feelings.

So what is this money that today has probably as powerful a role in human affairs as religions did in the past?

Some aspects of money have already been discussed in earlier chapters. It is a subject that could fill a complete book in itself, and even then give only a one sided view. Here it might be helpful briefly to give something of its nature, how it affects our thoughts and some of the healthy and unhealthy effects it can have on social life. Suggestions as to how we can work with it will be given in the second part of this book.

A look at how it evolved and its relationship to human awareness can be revealing. But it should be remembered that here we are talking about money which has arisen through the economic process of division of labor. In our present system money, or monetary value, also comes about through the rise of the monetary value of "rights," such as in the buying and selling of land, shares, options, and quotas. The money that arises in this way is not easily distinguishable from that which arises through the normal economic process, but it does have harmful consequences on the health of society. Although this will be briefly touched on later in this chapter, this is not the place to go into it at length.

The Evolution of Money and the Focus of Consciousness

Until very recently what was used as, and thus became, money was itself an economic product that had value in itself. Gold and silver are the obvious examples, but other metals as well as products, such as tobacco, have been used as money at different times and places. A simple example of this can be seen in the old English "penny." Gold and silver were originally measured in "troy" weights - 5760 troy grains made up one troy pound. 24 grains was a penny weight. A penny weight of silver became also a penny of money. 12 pennies were a shilling and 20 shillings a pound – that is, one pound of silver by weight was one pound value in money. So when a person sold something he had made, he received in exchange something that had value in itself, the silver in the form of a coin. The coin was worth its content of silver, and silver its weight in coins.

In purchase and sale there was then far greater consciousness of the value of what was given and what was received. By value is meant not the monetary value, but the intrinsic value that arises out of the process of production on the one side and the needs of the person buying it on the other. We can say that the focus of consciousness was on the value of the two things exchanged and their reciprocity. The products of labor were, of course, much simpler and the activity involved in their production more transparent than they are today.

At the next stage what happened was this. People did not find it convenient or safe always to carry their silver or gold about with them, so they stored it with a goldsmith or other "bank." They received from the goldsmith a receipt. At a later date these receipts were issued in the form of a bearer promissory note - "I promise to pay the bearer on demand the sum of...." These words still appear on all United Kingdom bank notes.

People then came to use the receipts as money rather than the actual silver. But now something was needed that was not necessary before - confidence. There had to be confidence in the receipt, that is, the person receiving it had to be confident that there was actual silver behind the receipt and that he could collect it if and when he needed it.

The next stage is a very important one that transformed the nature of money and brought about our present financial system.

The "bankers" up to now had issued a note of receipt only on the actual receipt of new coin, that is, of silver or gold, etc. The total number or value of the receipts issued and in circulation was the same as the amount of silver in the vaults. But the bankers came to see that, so long as there was confidence in the system, people did not come to collect their silver, but traded the receipts. There was never more than a small fraction of the deposited silver, somewhere around 10%, actually taken out at any one time. That is, nine tenths of the silver remained permanently in the bank.

The bankers came to realize that so long as they retained enough actual silver in their vaults to meet the needs of anyone wishing to withdraw their deposits, it would be possible to lend out at interest some of the nine tenths which was never collected, to anyone who could use it profitably. This would, of course, very much depend on people having confidence that they could always get their deposits when required and that the system remained stable.

What actually happened was that when the banker lent the silver to a borrower, the borrower handed the silver back to the banker (or to another banker within the banking system – the result comes to the same thing) and asked for a receipt. There were then more receipts in circulation than there was actual silver in the banks. The difference was made up by what was "owed" to the bank by the people who had borrowed the silver.

The next stage that came about during the first third of the twentieth century is that the silver (or gold) disappeared. That meant that people who held notes - money - receipts, could no longer go to the bank and ask for their silver. The paper receipt itself became the money, but an abstract money that had only a debt behind it. In the mean time the coins lost their silver content and had become "token" coins.

What started off as a "receipt" for actual silver or gold has now itself become money with nothing behind it but what is "owed" to the bank. It is now only partially in note form, and very largely nothing more than an entry in a book or a computer. The "I promise to pay the bearer on demand the sum of...."

has in most countries disappeared, or it has become a meaningless empty phase. The substance, even if only paper, has gone.

The consciousness that up to very recently looked for a balance of two values, the silver on one side and the product of a person's work on the other, now too often looks for the value of the product of human labor, not in the product itself, but in the numerical amount of the money asked as the price. Just when the money has lost all its substance and has become a complete abstraction, a number on a piece of paper, or an entry in an account book or a computer, we have come to focus most closely on it. We are increasingly determining values of all kinds, even sometimes of life itself, in terms of this money.

It should not be thought that this process of the evolution of money from substance to an abstraction has been a debasement of money or a deviation from its proper form and something that is itself detrimental to social life. On the contrary, this evolution or transformation is necessary and has been instrumental in creating the possibility of freeing human beings from the situation where the few can enjoy a cultural life at the cost of the labor of the many. But to achieve this possibility human beings have to become aware of the true nature of money and consciously take control of it.

Possibilities of Freedom

We have only to look into the past to see that up to quite recent times, and in many places still, the welfare of the whole community depended to a large extent on a division within the community. The members of one section of the community, much the smaller part, were free to develop their inner capacities, to be the leaders, the statesmen, teachers, priests, inventors, researchers, and the ones who strove for new horizons in all fields of human endeavor. But that this could happen, there had to be a much larger section of the community who labored at the nature base, at providing all the economic necessities of life. Those who labored on the land, in domestic service, and later in the factories and in the mines could not themselves take part in the active life of soul. This structure of society could satisfy only in so far as the old forms of community consciousness continued, where the individual still experienced himself as fulfilled, not out of his own inner striving and development, but out of that of the whole community, based on the blood relationship.

But with the emerging of the consciousness of individuality, this could no longer suffice. It is the freeing of money from its substantial basis that makes this division no longer necessary. As we saw earlier, it is money in the form of capital that enables human creativity to enter into the economic process. It is this creativity, human ingenuity, and the capacity for invention that has given the possibility of transforming the economic sphere to one that can provide for all and which can sustain a rich and soul fulfilling cultural life within reach of everyone, without anyone having to give up all their lives to toil and labor. Economically, there is no reason now for anybody to be hungry, homeless, cold, or without some access to a life of culture, nor is it necessary for anyone to labor at unfulfilling employment all his working life.

It is money working throughout economic life, and between the economic and cultural spheres that makes this possible. But there is also something required from the human being himself that he is not yet ready to provide: that is altruism, or brotherhood.

That is one aspect of money. It gives the possibility of freedom from toil to every human being. But what could be has not come about. Within the nature of money is also that which works destructively.

The Need to See through the Veil of Money

Money always has a tendency to hide the reality, to distort the truth. We see this in its most pronounced form in that humanity's attention has become focused on the substance-less money and has lost sight of what lies behind it, lost sight of the nature of the "value" that it stands for. The money itself has become a veil that has been cast over the actual economic process and hides all the human and natural activity that provides for the needs of the body and the soul during life on earth.

It is essential that this masking tendency be perceived. But it seems that few people have really grasped the seriousness of the situation. Without doing so we will never be able to work with money in a healthy way and to bring a healing to social life.

What is of greatest importance today is that we learn to see through money to what is the actual reality of social life: the activity and the human labor that lie behind even the simplest things that we use, the gifts of Nature and of God to which all people have an equal right, and what can emerge out of the freed human soul that itself must be free.

What Is It that Lies behind the Money?

It may help to give an example of what is meant.

Imagine a carpenter makes a table. This will involve a certain amount of work to complete all the activity necessary to make and finish it. He sells the table and receives money in exchange. He then decides that he needs a coat, and he buys one from the tailor. In paying for the coat, he hands over the money he received for the table.

Now another situation. A student is given a grant to enable him to study medicine. He must, of course, protect his health, and he finds that he needs a coat. He buys one from the tailor with some of the money he has been given as a grant.

Now a third situation. A person owns a house with a big garden in an area where it is difficult to get permission to build any more houses. But despite this, he applies for permission for a second house on his land, and his request is granted. As a result his land goes up in value, and he sells it at a profit. He decides he can afford a coat and goes to the tailor to buy one. To do this, he hands over some of the money that he made as profit on the sale of the land and receives in exchange the coat.

In each of these examples we see the money that was paid to the tailor as the same. What difference can there be in one lot of $200 from another $200. It is always just $200. On one level, that is, of course, quite true. But if we only see the $200, we do not see the social reality that is hidden behind it. So what is it that lies behind the money in each case? What is the social situation?

Behind the money the carpenter gave the tailor was the table that he had made; the table was the product of his work that he had passed over to the community. The money was a sign of this, that he had contributed something to the community. He received back in exchange something that others in the community produced and that he needed.

But what lay behind the money the student gave for the coat? He himself had produced nothing. But what of the future?

The student may well become a doctor and heal many people. In the future he may well benefit the community. There behind the money is the act of the freeing of the future potential in the student.

What lies behind the money which arose as profit on the land? He contributed nothing out of his own activity to the community. Nor is there anything implicit in the exchange that he would do so in the future. He receives a product of the work of the community but gives nothing in exchange. In this case the "profit" arose out of the permission that the community itself gave. Something that should properly belong to the sphere of rights has been "sold" as though it were an economic product.

It is a matter of consequence to the social life of the community that there are transactions where nothing is given in exchange for the product of other people's labor. This will have its effect on the social life of the community, even if it is not easily seen.

It means that instead of rights to such things as land and other forms of ownership being determined by the rights life itself, they are now largely allocated by purchase and sale. So "rights" have become "economic values" that lie behind much of the money in circulation. This distorts and plays havoc with the proper working of the economic process itself. This factor, though of very great importance, cannot be fully gone into within the scope of this book.

That is one aspect of the nature of money – that it has the tendency to coerce people to focus on itself and to mask what lies behind it.

The Corrupting Voice within Money

Now we will look at something that we can say lies within rather than behind money. To illustrate this I will give a personal experience. I am sure that anyone who has closely observed him or herself will recognize similar experiences in his or her own life.

Many years ago I inherited some money that I was not expecting. I really had no idea that I would one day receive this money. It was not a great amount, but I felt considerable gratitude for it. It meant we as a family could do something that we could not otherwise have done. After looking at a number of options we decided to build a room on to the house. The money was just enough for this. When the room was finished, it was a great improvement to the house, and we all felt thankful.

But I did come to see certain other small improvements that it would have been nice to get done at the same time, if there had been more money. Then I became aware of something in myself. Whereas I had been very grateful for the gift, for being able to build the room on to the house, now I found myself becoming almost resentful that it had not been more. When I realised this, it pulled me up with quite a shock, and I tried to look into myself to see what had actually happened.

I became aware of something like a voice, something that whispered, "What if it had been more?" It was a very persistent thought that I felt had been put into my head. "What if it had been more?" I saw all that I could have had, what money could do for me, if it had been more.

It would have been so easy to have slept through this event and not to have been conscious of what it was that entered into my thinking. It was just as though it came from outside, that someone had whispered it in my inner ear - what could have been done with more money? How often does such a voice whisper to us, and we remain asleep to our hearing it?

In the lectures on the *Fifth Gospel*, Rudolf Steiner points to the fact that Ahriman will always have access to us through money. And it his whisper one hears - "What if it had been more?"

There is always inherent in money the temptation to want more, to have something for nothing. Money can offer a life of ease, of not having to work. It gives us power to do what we want, to have control over others. It can take hold of us in such a way that it distorts all our better impulses and feelings. One can often see this in the area of gambling or the lottery. It is most active where there is money that is not "earned," that is, where there is nothing behind it, where someone has it but has given nothing back. It can play havoc within families, when there is any possibility of a dispute over inherited money.

Money Gives Personal Identity and Motive for Work

There is an increasing tendency for people to see the money they are paid as giving them a certain identity or dignity. To not be paid for work, or to be paid less than "the going rate," implies a loss of their personal worth.

I knew someone once who worked for a particular organization that could not pay him what he could expect for the same work elsewhere. But he wanted to work in that particular organization and what was offered was enough for him to live on with reasonable comfort. So he agreed to work for that salary. But after a while he could not continue. In the course of his work he would meet others in the same profession as himself.

Although they could not know that he was paid less than themselves, he did, and it gave him a feeling of inferiority, of loss of worth.

There are very many people who feel something of this. Some find it actually difficult to work, if they are not paid for the work. It is almost as though it is the payment of money which switches on the motive to work.

These are tendencies that can increasingly be perceived, particularly in people in the developed economies.

In Institutional Life

Anyone involved in discussions and decision making, particularly in such areas as salaries, wages, and budgets, needs to take all these aspects of money into account. If one is not awake to it, Ahriman will be there in the circle with you. His is a powerful force that can break a community apart. Something of these influences will always be there when money is involved, often below the level of consciousness, in some form or other in the feeling, in the thoughts, and in the willing of people. One can truly feel the reality of what Rudolf Steiner said in that Ahriman will always have access through money.

So, in money we have the possibilities of both good and evil. Humanity has to choose between the two.

I was once told that Ahriman is the spiritual banker. He likes to favor his own, but like all Spiritual Beings he has to obey the spiritual rules. If he is presented with a "good check," he has to pay. The question is, what is a good check?

Chapter Nine

Three Meetings

Each of the three spheres of social life must be free to act according to its own particular nature and laws. In each sphere the necessary meetings or supervisory organs must be created to decide on and be responsible for those concerns that lie within that sphere. Each of these organs will be different in character and function according to the nature of the sphere which it serves.

A look at the main characteristics of each of these three types of meetings or decision making bodies will also help to give further insight into the nature of each of the three spheres of social life.

Each has a different and individual gesture, which can approximately be shown by three forms. But it must be remembered that these must not be seen as giving a complete picture of the functions and forms of the meetings. They are, so to speak, true from a certain two dimensional perspective and can be very helpful as a guide to the working of the different meetings.

Any institution or organization will have a main purpose - as a school has to teach - that places it primarily into one or other of the three spheres of social life. But every such organization has each of the three spheres within it. So each of the following three forms apply in differing degree and purpose to all organizations.

Cultural Life

In cultural life we are always led to the single individual human being. We are led to the particular destined task, the capacities and uniqueness of each person. Some are gifted in one way, others in another. Some have outstanding capacities, while in others what they have is not always visible. For each one there is a different path through life. Each must find his or her own way, perhaps with guidance, but in freedom. Each must bring to fruition, and work out of, those capacities and intentions that they prepared in worlds of spirit before birth.

Each person must arrive at the truth for him or herself. Others might point the way, even explain it or try to convince them by pointing to certain truths, but a person can only know something when they have themselves confirmed it for themselves. They should only accept what another tells them as valid when they have satisfied for themselves the basis, the inner authority, on which the other speaks.

This is true of every person in so far as they are active or participate in the cultural sphere of social life.

In a meeting of people within cultural life the individual must always remain sovereign. Democracy, or the acceptance of the authority of the majority, will have no place. A good example of a meeting within cultural life is the College of Teachers of a

Waldorf school. Each teacher will bring to the meeting that which he has himself experienced, insights that he has arrived at. If a teacher is to act differently as a result of what is said by others in such a meeting, it must be because he has himself, after listening to the experience and thoughts of his colleagues, come to see its truth for himself, or that he sees that they speak out of experiences and insights that he has himself not yet had, but which he recognizes as valid.

Each individual human being is something like a star from which light shines forth, and the group or meeting is a constellation of different stars. That which lives and works in each, the qualities and impulses of each, shine forth and lighten the whole. But each also needs the light of the others, and each can be a mirror to the other.

Any authority that an individual acquires will be given due to the recognition by his colleagues of the wisdom, experience, or capacities of spiritual perception that he has come to within a certain field of work. Such authority will only extend as far as each individual freely recognizes and acknowledges it. Similarly, the authority of a meeting can only arise by the recognition of the capacities of the individuals that make up that meeting. A decision "by the meeting" can only be arrived at when, after discussion, the individual members recognize and agree to what is proposed by those they themselves see as having authority in the particular field under discussion.

Here we see each member as an individual, as a center within themselves. The meeting can only be a meeting of individuals and must decide matters on that basis.

Rights Life

In looking at the decision making organ of the rights life we must bear in mind that what we experience today as "government" or the "state" is very far from what it would be in a community or society that formed its organs on the basis of its threefold nature. In our present conceptions of social life, government is seen as the organ which, ultimately, is responsible for all three spheres of social life.

What we are trying to picture here is an organ of rights life, whether that is the government, an organ of government, or a committee within an organization that is responsible for, and whose powers are limited to, the bringing of order and the establishing of social law or rules of conduct, based on that which arises out of the common feeling life of the community.

In the rights sphere of social life the individual nature of each person must remain hidden. It is there necessary to become conscious, and work out of, that which is equal in every human being, not that which is different. Laws, rules, and the ordering of community life must arise not on a basis of what some people think is right or good for the community, not out of the authority or expertise of the few, but out of what lives as the common or prevailing opinion of all those who make up the community.

An organ of rights life will be one where the members try always to form the laws, regulations, and guidance of social life according to their sense of what is so willed by the members of that community which has elected them for that purpose. On the one side, they are a sense organ that senses what, out of a common feeling, is expressed as common opinion or will. What they thus sense, they must recast into laws or regulations that truly express what is willed by the community. Their responsibility and authority will, of course, apply only within that area where the common opinion or will is the valid basis of decision making.

The members of such an organ or committee may be there as representatives of one part of the community, but what arises as law or rules must be a reflection of what lives in the community as a whole. Even if members feel they have a connection with only a part of the community, they will work on the basis of a responsibility for the whole, not to look after the interests of just their section of the community. It is not what they personally feel or think to be right that is important. Their task is to listen to what is willed by the members. They are an instrument of the community by which that which is willed out of the feeling life is brought to expression as law or agreement. It is the common or majority opinion of the community that must be the basis for their decisions.

The members of the group would be appointed on some basis that reflects the will of the community, through some form of democratic process where every member can express his or her feelings and preferences. Each person within the community must be able to feel: "the members of the committee are placed there through a process in which I was involved. I could have my say and be heard on an equal basis with others. I am, therefore, content to abide by their decisions."

The group, or committee, would have authority to make the rules or laws that, in their opinion, best reflected the opinion of the community. There may be times when it is appropriate to set up other bodies to enforce those laws.

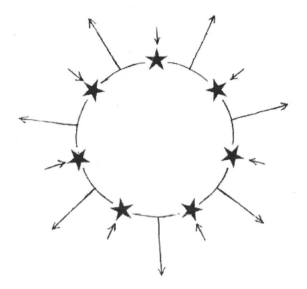

Here we see each member as a sense organ, one that hears or senses that which lives in the community. But, based on this, it is the group or committee that will formulate the laws, regulations, and agreements that bring order into that community.

Economic Life

In economic life we have seen that, unlike in the cultural sphere, the single person alone can achieve nothing. Nor, as in the rights sphere, can we go by the common opinion. The sphere of economic production is so complex and intertwined that it is not possible for any individual to view or understand more than the small area in which he himself is involved. Here we must work out of a coming together of experts, people who have experience in the different fields, if we are to get any picture of the working of the economy in any particular area. The nature of economic life demands this.

Each brings their knowledge, their perception of the economy from the particular place at which they stand in it, out of their egoism. But we saw in Chapter Seven that only that which is born within the group and that can rise above the egoism of the individual, can awaken the "objective community imagination." So it is the group that must reach to the wider community, to the periphery and to view the whole from there. It is this group that will then make the necessary decisions out of the view of the whole, which each must then be guided by. This is the basis of what is often called "associative working."

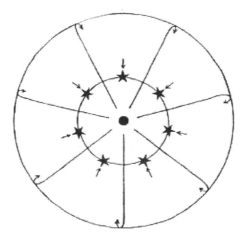

Here each member comes out his particular place within the economic sphere of social life, of his particular community or institution. He is there because he has certain expert knowledge or experience of the working of the economy. From within the group there can then arise what from the periphery perceives the economic life of the whole, and can also make those decisions necessary for it to work for the mutual benefit of everyone within the community.

This gesture, though primarily one for the economic sphere of social life as a whole, is also relevant for dealing with the economic affairs of any smaller community, such as a school or other cultural institution. There it may not warrant a separate group. The responsibility of the economic affairs may be carried by a committee or group that also has other responsibilities. What is essential is that the members must be able to change their "gesture" accordingly.

Conclusions

These three archetypal social organs are demands of all social or community life. Their separate working is demanded by the consciousness soul, and the realization of this will become increasingly critical as we move into the future.

In every community, organization, or institution, something of each of these three organs must be present and actively nurtured in some form, if the community is to be healthy. If any one is missing, or is not properly formed, then there will sooner or later be ill health in that community. Any one such organ can function in a healthy way only when the other two are also there in the community. The three can work separately only when they form a threefold unity. This is true for all communities and organizations, irrespective of which sphere of social life their work lies in.

It may not always be practical in a small institution to arrange separate meetings with different membership to deal with the concerns of each of the spheres. What is important then is that the members make a conscious transition from the dealing with the concerns of one sphere to that of another. They will need to adapt themselves to the appropriate form and mood in order to help them arrive at proper decisions.

PART TWO

Chapter Ten

Introduction

Up to now I have tried to give something of a picture of the threefold nature of social life as a whole. The threefold social order is, primarily, a description of human society and can only be grasped and worked with in the framework of the whole. Just as the school lies within and is a part of the whole, so its threefold nature will only be grasped when seen within the context of the whole. It cannot be grasped if looked at as separate and existing in itself. Only in that part of its activity that lies within the cultural sphere might an institution be able to develop some independence from society as a whole, but not in the rights sphere and even less so with regard to its economic needs.

Now, on the basis of what has already been discussed, I will try to give some ideas as to how it comes to expression in a school, college, or other anthroposophical cultural institution and how it can consciously be taken hold of in order to bring health and strength into the work and fulfillment to all who are involved in the school.

What I bring here is not intended as any sort of universal answer to problems or a set path to follow. It is put forward as a basis for study. It must always be remembered that, although the basic concepts of the threefold nature of social life are universally true, how they manifest in one organization or another, in one place or another, and in one time or another, can be very different, and the extent to which different individuals and groups can work with them varies considerably. The arrangements and structure that will succeed in establishing a healthy working in one institution will not necessarily work in the same way in another. In every person we meet we see the same threefold nature of body, soul, and spirit, and yet in each we meet a unique and distinct personality. So every institution is formed and functions on the basis of the same laws in its threefold nature, but in each the whole manifests differently.

As I pointed out earlier, my experience has been at Emerson College, a college of adult education. There are many differences between such a college and a school, but there are probably more similarities, and I do believe that much of what I have learned at Emerson may be helpful for others, even though they work in other kinds of institutions within cultural life. Some of what I set out here has been presented in one form or another in the various lectures and workshops that I have given to teachers, administrators, and board members in schools, mainly here in England and in America. Much of it will also be included in a more extensive book that I plan to write on the threefold nature of social life and on money for the public-at-large Anthroposophist as well as non-Anthroposophist.

I was a pupil for three years in a Waldorf school and latterly have worked with both teachers and administrators in such schools, but I, myself, have never worked in one, so I cannot speak out of direct experience. What I bring here is out of my experience at a college of adult education, so where necessary it will have to be translated into what is suitable for a school.

We are all, to a greater or lesser extent, conditioned in our thinking by the cultural life in which we live, by the thought forms that pervade and inform the social life of our time. The structure and conditions of our present society and institutions arise out of these thoughts. We cannot just change the outer forms, the structure and procedures, of our institutions, while we continue to think in the old way. If we do that, the new forms will break down, and the school may well find itself worse off than before.

If any change is to come, all those who work in the school must first recognize the necessity of bringing the form, constitution, and structure of the school into line with its actual threefold nature. In the Introduction to Part One, I gave several reasons why it is of vital necessity, if a school is to survive and fulfill its purpose, that it come to terms with the laws of its threefold nature. There is no doubt in my mind that many of the problems that schools are having to deal with, including the lack of more public support, arise out of the fact that at present this is largely ignored. The threefold nature of an institution is just as real as the threefold nature of the human being.

If there is to be development in this area, then all those who are involved in the school, and particularly those who carry responsibility, will need, step by step, to come to perceive this threefold being of the school and to understand something of its nature. Only then, gradually and methodically, can they begin to change things. Out of their working and studying together they will develop an imagination of what the school could be according to its true being, a goal that they intend to reach. That will then be there as something in the future, something that they strive towards. They must recognize that they can only work towards it. That is what is important, the development, the growing towards it. It may be slow, but it is the movement that is spiritually effective, not the speed, nor the immediate achievement of the goal. It is better to go forward slowly and get there than to rush ahead and crash.

The understanding and solving of social questions are not something that can be left to "the experts." Nor is it a question only for those involved in the administration or business side of the school. The social forms and structure cannot be imposed on a group of people working together. It will survive only if it arises out of the way those people feel and think. If those feelings and thoughts are healthy and true to the spiritual social archetypal phenomenon, then the school will develop a healthy structure; otherwise, sickness and disorders will live in the school's social structure. If people think or feel that they are employed by the school, that they are paid to work, then the social structure of employer/employee will live in the school. If they feel and think that what they receive as pay frees them to do their destiny work within this circle of colleagues, then a quite different social life and form will come into being.

This development will effect the relationships between people on all three levels. Freedom, equality, and brotherhood must all be nurtured, each in their own and proper place. I will attempt to look at the life of the school from the perspective of each of the three areas of its being.

For reasons that I will give later, and for simplicity, I will refer to all those who work in a school or college as "staff" or as "colleagues." They can be differentiated as teaching staff or administrative staff.

Intuition in the School

In the manufacturing process we can know the result of what we do. We decide the specifications of something that we want to make and then set up a series of actions that will result in the article that we set out to produce. If it does not turn out as we planned, we go back over our process to see where we went wrong and make the necessary adjustments. We start with an idea of what it is we want, and then we have to imagine the whole process through which it can be made, be brought into being. In the final product we can know with our ordinary senses what it is and how it came into existence. There is nothing "occult" about it. This is true of all products of economic activity, that is, of the products of manufacture, not necessarily of the actual substances and forces that are first taken from nature and then used in, or to make, the product.

In rights life we have to develop a sense of what is felt in the community to be right or wrong, just or unjust. In establishing a framework of law for social life, it is not a question of what any particular individual feels or comes to sense but of the common opinion.

It is not so in cultural activity. Consider education. It is a complete denial of the soul/spiritual nature of the child or young person, if we think we can decide what it is we intend her to become and then plan the education to achieve that end. Nor can we arrive at a proper form of education by listening to the common opinion, by sensing what is felt by the majority to be right or wrong.

There is a great deal that is hidden in the child, as she or he stands there before the teacher. How the child will develop, what will transpire as her life's work, and what will come to expression only in later years are not visible to the ordinary senses of the teacher. It is something that is prepared by the incarnating human being while still with the guiding Spirit Beings in the spirit worlds before birth and is brought into this life as intention or resolve, as potential. To be able to see this the teacher has to develop powers of intuition, that is those powers needed to perceive what it is that is not yet present, but that wills to come about in the future.

This is not only true of the child, but also of the teacher. How can one know what will come about if one invites a particular teacher to join the school? What are the karmic consequences of inviting a particular person to join their destiny to that of the school? How can we know of any children, though unconsciously, who may be waiting to see if a particular teacher will take a class, because their destiny lies with that person? If we take seriously that the child strives to find the teacher with whom she has a karmic connection, then we cannot say that with our ordinary senses we can perceive the consequences of inviting the one or other teacher. That we think a person to be a good or bad teacher, or perhaps to have characteristics that will not fit comfortably into the school community, though important, is not enough. We must also look beyond to what is potential, to what are the destiny initiatives that the individual brings with schools, but I myself have never worked in one, so I cannot speak out of direct experience. What I bring here is out of my experience at a college of adult education, so where necessary it will have to be translated into what is suitable for a school.

This is the essential nature of the school and of cultural life. It is always concerned in some way with bringing into being that which is not yet there in earthly life, to searching out the spiritual truths that are not immediately perceptible to earthly senses.

This can only be done in freedom. If a teacher teaches for money, if she does it because she is paid to teach, then she is not free. She will not be able to draw on that intuitive capacity that alone can fructify her work. Unless her activity is a free expression of her inner impulses and of her life's task, this soul faculty will withdraw from her, and her work will become mechanical. This is true of all work which we can say belongs to the cultural sphere of social life.

Chapter Eleven

Freedom and Individuality
in the Realm of the Soul

The Purpose of the School

What is the purpose of the school? Is the purpose seen as being to teach children, to bring Waldorf education to as many children as it can properly do so? This might seem as an unnecessary question to which the answer is obvious. But is it? I have met a number of schools where there has clearly been an underlying assumption, though not made conscious, that one purpose of the school was to be a "community," as much for the benefit of the staff as for the children. It is very important that the purpose of the school, the reason for its existence, be consciously seen to serve the children.

When a group of people come together in order to work towards the fulfilling of a need that is beyond themselves, then community will arise. To the extent that the group focuses their attention on the work to be done, the serving the needs of children, then community will of its own accord come into be-ing. But so far as the focus of the intention, of the purpose of the coming together, switches from the work to the "being a com-munity," then a sickness manifesting as division, discord, and disharmony will enter the school.

That leads to another and more important question:

"Why Am I Doing This?"

Every person who works in a school, whether her work lies in the realm of teaching, in the office, or elsewhere, should at some time ask herself the question: "Why am I doing this? Am I doing it out of an impulse that lies within my own soul, or am I impelled to it out of some other need? Am I doing it in order to earn a salary, or does the salary make it possible for me to do what I have to do, what I am led towards out of those resolves I set for myself as the work of this incarnation?"

It is really of very great importance for the ongoing strength of the school that those involved come to a quite con-scious recognition in their own minds of the answer to this question.

This is not an easy question to answer. We have to first penetrate through all those concepts that we take in from out-side, from the social environment in which we live, both as chil-dren and as adults. We are not always aware to what extent our way of thinking, our concepts, opinions, and moral judgments are given to us out of the social group into which we are born and in which we grow up and live. Very often we think they are our own, but they are what we have inherited out of this social environment. In this we are not free. We cannot be free, unless we first recognize what it is that governs our thoughts and ac-tions from outside and replace this with that which we bring out of ourselves through our own activity.

I remember the time, in my early thirties, when I came to the terrible realization that what arose in me as thoughts, feelings, impulses, judgments, and decisions did not come from me, out of my own activity. I came to the conclusion that some ninety-five percent of the decisions I made, of the judgments I came to, were due to the social environment in which I was brought up. They came from the fact that I was born and brought up a "Spence," a white, colonial, upper middle class, English, male. I felt that no more than a fraction were my own as a free conscious individual human being. That discovery came as a considerable shock and was one of the main impulses that led me to the meaning of Anthroposophy.

One such thought that we take in from our social environment, and widely assume to be true, is that we work in order to earn money on which to live. This thought over-shadows what many then do not see, that in reality they actually have a certain inner need to do just what they are doing. We each have to get through to the reality of our destiny impulses. Then we might see the real motivation out of which we work. Many of us will find that we do the work we do, because we need to do it, that the need for the work arises from within ourselves.

We will then come to the realization that "only by doing this work to the best of my ability can the meaning and purpose of my life be fulfilled."

The conscious realization of this will become one of the foundation stones on which the future development of the school can be built.

There are a number of ways in which these questions can be worked with and a conscious realization of the answers be strengthened. For example, one possible way is to openly discuss in the staff circle the question of destiny and karma and how this manifests in our lives. Is karma recognized as a fact in our lives, do we know it to be true, or is it nothing more than a belief that does not survive the light of everyday reality? At Emerson we often started each weekly staff meeting with one member speaking to a thought such as "I and Emerson College." Everyone did this, one person each week. They could speak for five minutes in any way they liked around this thought - what brought them to the College, how were they met, what it means to them now to be here, what is fulfilled in themselves to be here. They did not have to say anything they did not want to say, and nobody had to do it. We also worked with other thoughts, such as "the festivals and I." This way of beginning a meeting was always appreciated by all involved and was greatly strengthening of the social bonding of the colleagues. One constantly came to the perception that the speaker was not accidentally in the circle; there was a certain orderliness about it.

There are individual experts and organizations who can advise far better than I can on how a group can work with such questions as to how to awaken a perception of the reality of karma in a group.

If a person working within cultural life cannot answer the question other than to say she is working to earn money, then a situation has come about which, if left unattended, will eventually lead to conflict.

It may, of course, be that she is in her right work, but that she has not been able to free herself from the prevailing thought forms, and so she thinks that she is working to earn money. Another possibility arises out of present social conditions, which mean that many souls have very great difficulty finding their way to and recognizing their real work. This may not be her intended work, but the nearest to it she can find.

And those who do find their way are often so handicapped by the education they received and the social convictions of today that they cannot realize their own skills and capacities, nor see their own true intentions.

Many people go through several areas of work in their lifetime. Some jobs at the beginning of life might be no more than a preparation for the real work later on. But then also a person can stay beyond her time in one place; she may need help and encouragement to take her next step.

But anyone working in the cultural sphere of social life and who is in her right place and work according to her own karma should eventually be able to recognize this. It is essential that she do so. If she fails to do this and continues to think that she is working to earn money, she will constantly develop false relationships to her work, her salary, between herself and her colleagues, and between herself and the world.

Do I See the Other Person?

The next step is to ask ourselves how we see our colleagues. Do we see also in them a destiny basis for their work in the school? Do we consciously see and know that each is placed in his or her work through the working of karma and that each brings something different that is needed by the school, that there is a reason for his or her being in the school that is deeper than can be seen on the surface?

When we meet another person, what do we actually see? When we walk down the street and meet another person, perhaps a policeman, who is it that we see? Do we see just a policeman and assign to him all the preconceived concepts we have of "policeman"? Or do we see the individual human being who has put on the uniform and taken on the work of that which is needed by society, the policeman? Can we see through the uniform, through the function, to the individual human being? Do we recognize in him, too, the working of destiny and karma? In him, also, there are those resolves and impulses that come from the life before birth and from previous incarnations. It makes an enormous difference if we see a person as a unique and individual human being, or as only a function, labeled with general and preconceived concepts that apply to the job. The individual herself will then feel that her humanity is denied. There may have been some justification in looking at another person in that way in earlier times, when people experienced themselves as members of, and fulfilling a task within, a family group united through the blood. But it is injurious to the person of today, as she awakens to the consciousness of herself as an individuality.

This is comparatively easy to understand with regard to a policeman, or someone in uniform. But we do this to each other. We label a colleague as a "teacher," "artist," "business manager," or "bursar," and do not see the individual human being. The most serious failure in this respect in cultural institutions is nearly always between those who teach and those who work in the office or other areas of administration. Many support staff feel they are seen as inferior human beings. I remember once being approached during a festival by a student with a question concerning his tuition fee account. I got angry and asked if I really had to deal with it during a festival. Four days later he came to see me to apologize. He told me he had come to realize that when he saw me, he "saw the $ sign."

The individual may come to recognize for herself that she is placed in her work in the fulfillment of her karma and of the those resolves she brought with her through birth. But do those within the circle of her colleagues also recognize it? This, I do believe, is a basic question for every school, and for every member of the staff circle.

We can put the question another way. When we employ or hire a person, what are we actually doing? Are we paying her to do certain work, determined and defined by us, the school, and given her in the form of a job description? Or do we recognize her karma, the impulses and capacities that live within her and that "gives her authority," and so invite her to join her work with ours, within the organizational forms and guidelines already created?

What do I mean here by "authority"? Can we recognize that a person, while still in the spiritual worlds during the time before birth, connects herself with certain work, perhaps just that work that also lies at the heart and the intentions of the school? During this time she prepares herself for this work according to that which is given her by her karma and in conjunction with the Beings of the spiritual world. She then incarnates with those resolves and capacities needed to enter into her work.

When we sit with our colleagues in the circle of a meeting, can we each recognize that the other, in so far as she is rightfully there, is placed there through karma, through the working of an all wise beneficial providence? It was not the school, or the board, who led her there. They enabled karma to be fulfilled - or not fulfilled.

If this thought really lives in each one in the circle, then it will also be recognized that there is a great deal about each one that cannot be known. We can only have trust that there is a purpose in each being there and have the courage to provide the free space for that purpose to be fulfilled, and to allow each to speak "with authority" in those areas in which she has such "authority."

Can we really tell her better how to do her work? Have we greater authority?

When a colleague has an initiative - proposes a new way of doing something, or wishes to do something that has not been done before - do we judge it from our own stand point, from our own way of thinking and opinion, from what we like or dislike, or do we look to the authority within the initiative itself, that authority that speaks through the initiator?

Of course, we must help and encourage each other to awaken and bring out of ourselves that which lies deep in the unconscious depths of our being, often overlaid and hidden by so much that has come from the education we received and the social environment in which we live. We must be able to give and take advice, to be something of a mirror, to reflect back to each other that which the other is and does, and what she can become. But there must always be the recognition of what is there in the innermost depth of each human being and which has to be brought to realization.

Only on a basis of this individual freedom can cultural life be what it must be, if the human soul is to be nourished and allowed to work and grow and the purpose of earthly life be fulfilled. This freedom has to be given by the community to each individual.

Of course, much or most of this we know already. But do we know it? Or do we "know" with our heads, but act on concepts and thoughts that are different from what we "know"? Does it actually live in each colleague sitting in the circle of the teachers, faculty, staff, or board meeting? When we hear a colleague proposing a course of action with which we disagree, do we listen to her in the sure knowledge that there is in her that which works out of the depths of her resolves and intentions formed in worlds of spirit, and in which this proposal may have its roots? Or do we just know that we disagree with her, and that we must convince her?

People act out of what lives in them, out of what they have taken hold of within themselves, not out of what they have taken in as theory, or been told is right action, or how they ought to behave, or out of what has been established as given structures and rules. A school will have life and creative vigor, when those who form its carrying body recognize and know as an absolute truth, not only in their heads, but in their feelings and their will, that only out of the working in individual freedom can that which is a need of our time come into being in a living way.

This is a second foundation on which the further development of the school can be built.

Examples of the Working of Karma

If we carefully and objectively observe life, we will find very many instances of just this, of situations that can only be explained by a recognition of the working of karma and of those deep resolves we each of us carry into life.

Let me give out of my experience three different examples of where something below the surface was at work. It would be possible to bring very many more. (In order to respect the privacy of the individuals concerned, I always feel it necessary to bring such examples in a way that does not make it easy to identify them.)

We once had to make a decision as to whether to commit ourselves to the expenditure of taking on a new teacher to take over an existing course. The course had shown signs of decline for some years. Student numbers were dropping, and there was a question as to whether it would be better to close it. But there was a particular individual whom we were interested in inviting to take over this course, but to do so we had to make a considerable financial commitment, a commitment that outwardly could be seen as too risky. But the decision was made, and he joined the College.

Looking back later I observed that after the decision was made to take on the new teacher, but before this was advertised or generally known, there already appeared an increase in new applications for that course, and the numbers of students in the course grew substantially. The question I asked myself - were these new students waiting, in the unconscious depths of their souls, for the decision to be made, because that was their teacher? Did they "know" when the decision was made?

Of course, this could have been a coincidence. But I have seen this kind of thing too often to be able to accept them all as coincidences. There is too often a kind of logic to them. They make sense of the idea of karma and of the recognition of a spiritual world out of which we come and to which we are still connected.

A second example. Some years ago a mature man came to the College as a student. He did not find it easy to be a student. There was in him a strong impulse to help deprived people in a particular way, and soon he talked about himself starting a course, which for many reasons he wanted to have at Emerson. It was not easy to contain what was experienced as a strong impulsive individual, but the College did support him in his intentions, and he started the course, which attracted much interest. But things did not go easily, and there were always financial problems and often personality clashes. Being on the council of management and various committees, I myself was very involved in working with him to see that the course was viable and kept within certain limits. I had many clashes with him. I often experienced that there was a disharmony between his head, his heart, and his impulses. Having to a certain extent got the work here going, he left to carry it further elsewhere.

Though I had many difficult times with him, I came to like and to respect him deeply. It was as though there were two quite distinct aspects to him. There was he himself, a very likable and gentle individual who deeply cared about others. Then there was the impulse that lived deeply and powerfully in him and that impelled him to action.

As I came to know him, I became convinced that there lived in him a very real impulse that he had brought with him through birth from out of the spiritual worlds. This impulse was something that actually was of great importance and was needed in the world. But somehow it was not able to work properly. There were inconsistencies and distortions in the way it came to expression. I became convinced that if he had had a proper Waldorf education, if as a child he had lived in a social environment where such impulses could be properly allowed to develop, then he would have been able to achieve what he had, in the life before birth, resolved to do. Deep down, buried under so much of the garbage of modern materialistic thinking, there was indeed a true impulse brought from out the spiritual worlds.

Again a different example: Some years ago two young men came to the college. Although they came from different parts of the world and had not met before, there soon developed a strong friendship between them. They started to miss classes, and after a time it seemed that they were spending more time in London together than in the class. Despite discussions with them, the situation did not really improve. Although they both had access to funds, neither had paid their fees, including the cost of room and meals for the term.

It seemed obvious they should be asked to leave; they were not properly attending the course and had not paid their fees. Then the question was put forward, "Why had they come? What had led these two young men to decide to come to Emerson College?" There was no apparent answer to this question, nor were they obviously irresponsible young people. There was no evident outer reason why they should have chosen to come here, if in fact they did not want to be here. So why? There must be a deeper reason. Surely their destiny had brought them here, and their everyday consciousness had not yet been able to see what it was they had come for. The distractions were too great. If their destiny had brought them here, then there must be a reason for that. It was up to us to work more deeply with the situation.

The teachers concerned did have to be firm with them and give an ultimatum. Then they did take hold of themselves and attend the course, and they paid their fees. Both went on to do good and important anthroposophical work. Here was a wonderful example of how the real impulse that motivates a person can easily be missed behind the more apparent and quite different outer actions. It is those deeper underlying intentions which we need to recognize and in which we must have confidence.

If we observe life, we really will see many such examples, even in our own lives.

Can We Give Karma a Chance?

I would like to give one example of how working with karma can help us work more efficiently. There are, of course, many.

Here at the College, as I am sure also at most schools, we periodically find we suffer from too many meetings that go on for too long. What can often happen in such as the weekly staff or faculty meeting is that a question comes up which needs a decision and that affects a number of people who all have something different to say. For example, a question comes up as to whether a certain initiative for a weekend activity may take place. It will affect a number of people and a change of use of rooms. Does this activity fit into and have a relationship to the work of the College, and is it important enough to justify the disturbance of other activities that will result, and if so how can this be minimized? This will be discussed for sometime, with all the possibilities and problems and alternatives being aired.

There are a number of possible ways of dealing with such a question. One is to talk it through to a decision. If the meeting is above a certain size, what will often happen is that the discussion goes on, until out of exhaustion a decision is come to, but one that may well be questioned at a later meeting, and probably have to be talked through again. Or what can also often happen is that such questions are left to the same few individuals, who then tend to run the college or school. They are overworked, which means that a certain stagnation can enter the institution. Or it can be left to one of the existing committees; for many questions that might well be the right way forward. But there are always those questions which stand out, needing special attention and which do not belong to any existing committee. It is also good to handle questions in different ways and not to pass everything to established committees.

What now often happens here is that when the discussion reaches a certain point, someone will suggest that it has been discussed long enough, and everyone has had a chance to express their views. Then there is a proposal of something to the effect that X, Y, and Z seem to be connected to the question, or have given it some thought, or even have strong opposing views. They have heard what we all think. Why not leave it to them to work through the question and come back and tell us their decision?

Life has shown that everyone has depths of hidden wisdom, not just the few or the "wise" ones, and that if we listen carefully when someone speaks who does so out of deep feeling and will for the question, then we can know when to have the confidence to give the freedom and responsibility to that person or people to deal with the situation. The confidence must be such that what she or they then decide is not later questioned and again discussed. Then there is the opening for the new, that which wills to come about out of the future, to unfold itself rather than only a continuation of the past.

Of course, mistakes can and will happen. We must not hold back out of fear of making them. They will happen anyway. We must learn from our mistakes; later they are opportunities for growth and development. The greatest mistake is to try to create a system where there is no freedom to make mistakes. A balance must be sought between that and one of allowing anyone to be involved in making the decisions, just because they want to, or because they represent a faction.

The recognition of the potential, the seed, that is in every human being, and giving it the freedom, the space, to blossom is something that needs constantly to be nurtured in every institution or community, if that community of work is truly to live.

We must learn to differentiate between an initiative that arises out of a person's own destiny work and one that arises, for example, out of her need to gratify her ego. That a person wants to do something does not itself justify her being given the freedom to do it. It is not easy to see what lies behind an impulse. But once we recognize that there do lie in the depths of human souls real impulses that are ones also needed by the school and humanity, then we can more readily come to a recognition of when to give freedom, and when not to do so.

All this can be more easily understood when seen in the context of the teachers. But it is important that it be recognized as true also of the other colleagues, those who work in the office, environment, or maintenance.

That which has to unfold for the future will do so, not out of studying the past through books, libraries, museums, or ancient works of art. All that is certainly important, and it will reveal a great deal to us, especially about the present. But the future, that which wills to come into being in the course of the further development of humanity, will do so out of individual impulses, through the unfolding in freedom of those impulses and resolves brought from worlds of Spirit. This is true of the life of the school, just as it is for humanity as a whole.

Only when we truly give each other the freedom to speak, and the space to act, out of what is trying to come to expression in the depths of each soul, will the future be able to unfold as it wills to and should. Only in that way can the school have life and vigor, and will it attract those souls who long to find a place where they can prepare to "remember their task," that is to find their way to act out of their pre-birth resolves.

Chapter Twelve

Equality in the Spirit

In a certain sense a school can be seen as a "community of works." A number of people have come together to serve a common vision. They have brought to the common task all their varied talents and abilities. The individual skills, training, and experience needed by the class teacher, the eurythmy or language teacher, the administrator, and gardener are all very different. It is just because the abilities and gifts that they bring are different that the common task can be achieved.

But these differences will divide and separate people. They will tend to create a hierarchical structure in which some are seen as more important or better people than others. A community of work will never arise out of that alone which separates people. There must be something also which unites them, which goes beyond the differences to that which is based on what is equal in all people.

We can look at this from a particular perspective. What is the purpose of the school, the reason why all the people have come together in a common task? Put simply, we could say that the purpose of the school is for the child to meet the teacher. The teacher and the school have a common purpose. The teacher finds her work. Her purpose in the work, and the purpose of the school are one. But is that true of the person working in the office? What is the nature and purpose of her work? Her purpose must also be in the child meeting the teacher, but her work is not that of the teacher. If we take away the meeting between the teacher and the child, there would be no purpose to the work in the office. The office has no purpose in itself. So how does the individual working in the office find her purpose? Ultimately, her purpose must be to make possible the teaching. So often, because she does not teach, the worker in the office is seen as a second class member of the community, one who is even looked down on by those whose work she makes possible.

To realize her purpose, that she is also one who carries the work of the whole, there must be something in the community that connects her to the central task of the school. If this is not achieved, there will always be a tendency to go one of two ways. Either she will do just what she is paid to do, no more; she will become a clock watcher, or else she will try to find a purpose in her own work. This will develop into the forming of a power base in the office, a management of the activities and development of the school through the establishment of bureaucratic or accounting control. This may be unconscious, but it can be there just the same, and once established extremely difficult to heal.

Every human being is unique and individual. People's capacities and skills vary considerably. Some can teach. Some are perhaps very good teachers who, on the basis of their wisdom are given a leading role in the school. Others cannot do that; they do not have those abilities that are especially important to the community. Some can do only the simplest tasks. These differences between people will separate and divide them, if there is not also something else which unites them. To achieve this we must see beyond the differences, the unique individuality of each to that which is equal in all people.

The person who works in the office, or who keeps the buildings in repair, makes it possible for the teacher to teach. She can want to do this and find her purpose in her work, when, in meeting the teacher she experiences as a reality that the teacher sees her as one who makes it possible for her, the teacher, to do her work. Her work is fulfilled when she recognizes that the teacher feels a sense of gratitude, and even of humility, before the person who works at a task that does not arise directly out of that person's own inner soul needs but that is done in order that the teacher can do the work that gives her inner fulfillment.

Whatever her unique qualities, or lack of them, each person needs to be able to feel that she is seen as a full human being, and as such she is of equal importance in the circle of colleagues, and that this is recognized by the whole circle. This is an essential counter balance to the separation and division that will otherwise occur between people due to their individual karma and capacities.

A person attends meetings, such as the teachers meeting, or is appointed to the Board or Council, due to their particular work or their individual capacities and experience. In such meetings a person is listened to, because she speaks out of her particular knowledge, experience, or work. Some people speak out of a deeper wisdom than others and will be listened to with greater attentiveness. It is very easy for others who do not have those capacities and are not able to achieve that wisdom to be made to feel inferior. In addition there are all too often those who work in a school, who do important work in supporting it, but who are not members of any regular meeting. They come to their work and then go home, without any contact with those whose work they support, except that which arises through the work itself.

In the realm of the soul every human being is unique and individual. Each one follows his or her own destiny. Each has her own individual path to tread and her own biography. But in the third member of the human being, in the spirit, there is that which is universal, that is equal in every human being. In every person of whatever nationality, religion, sex, social background, or individual capacities, there is in the innermost depths of her being something that is of the substance of the Divine. In this all people are equal. The recognition of this is an ever increasing demand of our time, a demand of the age of the awakening consciousness soul, of the awakening to one's own individuality. When we do indeed come to recognize it, we will find that it calls forth in us reverence for the innermost being of each person we meet. It is now important, and will become increasingly so in the future, that we create in our institutions and communities a place where this need is recognized and served.

There has to live in each member the consciousness that there is that in every colleague which makes them equal as well as that which makes them different. The recognition of the different and unique character of each individual, and also of that which is equal in all people, are two quite distinct demands of our time. The consciousness of these two demands must give rise to a structure in the school that serves these two needs of the human soul and which itself again supports and strengthens this consciousness. What lives in the individual and the structure of the school must be mutually supportive.

The Staff Meeting

One way to achieve this is to create a regular meeting of all those who work in the school. It must be one which people attend not out of any particular work or individual gifts but due only to the fact that they work at the school. They are a part of the community of work which is the school. It will be a meeting where, in that sense, they are on an equal level with everyone else in the circle, and the business of the meeting will be that which arises out of that fact. In such a meeting everyone, office workers, teachers, gardeners - all who work in the school - should feel they are there, because they are one of the circle of colleagues who carry the work of the school. The circle should be one which is felt to be incomplete if anyone, whatever his or her work, is missing. Even the one who does the simplest of work should be able to sense that there the others see her as an essential colleague without whom the school would not be as it should be. The individual should be able to say, "Here, in this circle I am one with my colleagues; I am seen and listened to as a colleague amongst colleagues."

It should not, in the main, be a decision making body, but one where information is shared, reports on work, new developments and initiatives given, where shared questions can be discussed. It should be a place where those carrying a common work can meet each other as people and can get to know what lives in the others as question or impulse. In my opinion, to be effective it needs to meet weekly alongside the other weekly meetings.

If it is to fulfill its role in creating a unity of the whole staff, as a balance to that which separates, it is essential that other decision making bodies, such as the Board or College of Teachers, give a regular picture to this meeting of the questions they are dealing with. Where possible this should be done before actual decisions are made. If, for example, the council reports that such and such a question or problem has arisen, that these are the factors as far as they can see and on which they will have to make a decision, then others not involved in the decision will, nonetheless, experience that they are included, that decisions are not being made by remote bodies and handed down. If someone does have thoughts on the matter, she knows that the discussion is taking place and that she can say something and be heard before the decision is made. What happens then is that instead of wanting to be involved in every decision, people are grateful that others take on the task and responsibility of making the decision.

Too often in schools and similar organizations, decisions are made by the appropriate body in isolation from the whole. The people concerned may take some time developing a policy, and perhaps talking to others who are directly affected. But the wider group does not know anything until after the final decision has been made, or they hear something by way of gossip. So there develops a "them and us" culture.

A healthy working together can only arise out of the actual recognition that everyone is a part of the whole, that the work and life of the school are a responsibility carried by all who work there, even those who are not themselves directly involved in making the decisions. Then each person not involved in the decision making will be happy that others are so involved, because she will know and feel that she herself is "seen." She is not excluded from the consciousness of those who do make the decisions. It makes a very great difference to the social life of the school, and, therefore, to the carrying of the work by the whole community, if the processes of discussion and decision making are accompanied by the whole. They do not all have to be actually involved, but they must be able to follow the process.

Such a weekly meeting has existed at Emerson College since the early days. In fact, it started before any of the other meetings, except the council meeting. This is the Staff Meeting. Its form has changed and continues to do so, but its basic purpose has continued. It meets every week, and everyone who works in an ongoing way at the College in whatever capacity is expected to attend. All people who work at the college are called "staff" - teaching staff, kitchen staff, office staff etc. This use of a common designation itself helps to establish a sense of colleagueship.

Any major changes, new initiatives or developments, also any crises that have to be resolved, wherever possible, will be brought to the staff meeting before being finally decided on. There might even be times when a matter is brought more than once, so that the progress of the discussion or development is shared and so carried with all staff. It can be discussed there, but everyone knows that it cannot be decided in the large staff meeting. That can only be done in a smaller group. In actual practice, most staff become very grateful to those who do give the time and energy that is needed for the decision making process. The staff will also be kept informed of any changes in the ongoing financial situation for the year.

It is a time when anyone who has been away to a conference or visit to somewhere interesting will report. We might share our thoughts and hopes for our individual work. Sometimes we take turns to talk about our area of work, what it means to work in the office or kitchen, what are the questions and the particular character of the students of each course this year.

As pointed out earlier, as our work is with adult students, we have no parent body. But we do have the student body. The parallel to the staff meeting in the College as a whole is the weekly house, or college meeting. How a school would include parents in this is not a question I have had to work with, but it is something that needs to be developed.

The New Member of Staff

Let us look at the kinds of actual situations that often do arise. Let us look, for example, at a school which has a need for a new member of staff. Let us suppose it is a eurythmy teacher. Perhaps the school has not previously had regular eurythmy, except what could be provided by visiting teachers. But now the question is raised as to whether a full time teacher should be taken on. Who makes the decision? The school cannot easily afford to increase its staff. Finances are tight, and salaries, while not desperate, are low and likely to continue below what everyone feels is reasonable. But there are those who feel strongly that the school must take a next step in its development, if it is to grow and become what it intends to become.

Clearly such a decision cannot be made democratically. It must be made by those who carry the vision and the teaching work of the school, those who are able to know the importance of eurythmy in the curriculum and what it means for the children to have or not have it. They must also be able to perceive something of the intentions and the karma of the individual who wishes to join the school. The financial implications will also have to be looked at by those who carry the ultimate financial responsibilities.

But what of those who are not involved in the same way as others are, those who work in the office, and the parents? Is the office worker just an employee who will eventually be told that a decision has been made? Is she expected to work and to be involved only so far as that for which she is paid? If that is so, then a certain kind of institution will arise, one that is divided, that does not nurture those forces that can only arise when all have a common vision towards which each in his or herown way strives.

The office worker needs also to have that imagination of the task of the school, to feel what it is she is a part of, what it is she helps to make possible and to which she can also put her "will." She needs this perhaps even more than the teacher, who does after all work with the children and finds a certain inner fulfillment in that work. The imagination of the work of the school, of what Waldorf education means not only for the children but also for the social needs of the world, must live in those who work in the office, just as in the teachers. If this is to live as the visible purpose of the office worker, just as of the teacher, and if this is to be a strengthening factor in the whole work and life of the school, every individual, whatever their work and "usefulness," must be recognized as having an interest in such an imagination. Then they, too, can take responsibility for the decision, although they were not themselves involved in making it.

Such a way of working together can only arise through an actual meeting of all concerned in something like a "staff meeting." All the written reports that can be produced will never achieve this.

In the staff meeting the need for the new teacher, together with the implications for the school, both positive and negative, can be put forward, what it will mean for the children and the financial consequences, etc. Some idea of the personality of the individuality, who may be invited into the circle of colleagues, should also be given. A new person coming in will affect the whole circle, and everyone should be able to accompany the decision. If this is brought forward in a spirit of sharing, it is surprising how often everyone will support whatever decision the council or whoever eventually comes to, and frequently people are only too glad that they did not have to be involved in making the difficult decision.

Each person in the community of work can "take responsibility" for a decision, although they were not themselves involved in the actual deciding, because the structure and decision making bodies of the school came into being out of the will of the whole. That is when each one can say, "It is as it is, because that is the way we have willed it. In this my voice was also heard, and, therefore, I join my will with the others." It brings enormous strength to an institution when each person who works in it can feel herself as one with the whole, and that the whole arises out of what lives in each individual.

What is "the school"? Is it the institution that exists in its own being and that employs the teachers and others whose work keeps it going? Each person will have their place within the institution and will do the work and make the decisions according to the needs of the institution. People will come and go as employees, but the institution will continue.

Or is it the group of people, the circle of colleagues, together with the children and the parents that "are the school" at any one time? The school will be the sum total of all the people involved, and it itself will change as people come and go. A consciousness of such matters will greatly help to establish a healthy and vibrant culture in the school. To be asleep to them brings a sleepy culture and allows those forces entry that wish to divert human development from its proper course.

The question must then arise, "How can we structure the school in such a way that in it each individual finds a living expression of what lives in her as impulse, finds also in it the summons to develop what is truly human within herself, and the school is also carried by the will and activity of every person who has a place in it?"

Chapter Thirteen

The Rights Sphere - Equality

As was pointed out earlier, the rights sphere of social life has a very particular nature that is quite different from both the cultural and the economic spheres. It is very important that in any organization something of this nature be understood and remembered. The rights sphere fulfills a very essential function in social life, but there is also always within it the potential for destructive forces to enter into the school. But first let me give a reminder of what we mean by the rights sphere. It is very easy for confusion to be experienced here.

In the last chapter we looked at what needs to be striven for by each individual member of the staff circle of the school. This is the recognition of, and the reverence for, what is the innermost and hallowed essence of each human being. It is equally there in every human being, in each child, in each parent, and in each colleague. This is something that can only come from each individual. It is not something that the community can establish.

But to the extent that people are not yet awake to the spiritual in each person they meet, they will not out of themselves always act socially towards others. So there is a need for what on an earthly level brings order into earthly community. This is what we refer to as the rights sphere. The equality demanded of the rights sphere should not be confused with that equality of all people in the spirit which is not of this earth. This duality was touched on in Chapter Four.

When we speak of the rights sphere of social life, we refer to that sphere which brings order and regulation into earthly community life to the extent that individual human beings cannot out of their own inner moral development act socially towards one another. It is something that belongs only to earthly life.

Just as we as individuals strive to recognize that which is of the spirit in each human being, so there always has access through the rights sphere, whether of the community at large or the individual organization, that which tends to deny the spirit, to bind us to the earthly. This is something that must be kept constantly in mind when making rules and regulations in a school. It is one of the areas to which, to my mind, not nearly enough attention is given in anthroposophical schools and institutions.

It is not possible to get around the problem by not having rules and regulations. There must be a structure. It is not enough to rely on the good intentions, of even the good people in whom we have every confidence. Very few of us have the strength to act always out of our good intentions under adverse conditions, particularly where such action would have a detrimental effect on our own interests.

Let us look at a simple example of the place of rights life in school. Take the situation where a school needs a new teacher, and there is one who applies to take up the position offered. At that point there is freedom on each side. Each has yet to decide whether to go forward or not. But there comes a moment when terms and working arrangements and responsibilities are agreed, and the decisions made. There is a contractual agreement. She takes responsibility for a particular group of children as their class teacher. The school agrees to pay her a certain amount and provide for her in other ways. Whether verbal or written, that is an agreement, a contractual arrangement.

It is no longer a free situation but is one bound by the agreement made between the new teacher and the school. The teacher cannot expect to have the freedom to decide on her own, whenever she may feel like it, to stop teaching her class and to start teaching sport to other children instead. Nor is the school free to decide arbitrarily to replace her with someone else they find they like better, without good cause as provided for in the agreement.

Some people might say that surely this would not happen, that teachers in Waldorf schools can be relied upon to act out of certain moral and social principles, and that there is no need for a contract. That might be true of 95% of them, but these and similar things have happened and will continue to do so. Our individual moral and social will is just not strong enough to be capable of maintaining the necessary order and social conduct in our actions. The conflict between being bound by an agreement freely entered into and the need for personal freedom can be too much for some people. There has to be something coming from outside to make up for this lack of moral discipline where that cannot be provided from within.

It is the rights life of the community that establishes order and ensures some sort of social stability. It fulfills a real need of the life of society. When all else fails, it is the only way left to prevent the free reign of the egoistic and anti-social forces in humanity. It, also, through the bringing of an ordered structure into social life, provides security and the space for freedom.

But this which must come from outside, from the rights sphere of social life, has also its dark nature. Through this rights life it is possible for certain adverse spiritual beings to gain entry and have influence over people and organizations and over the social life of humanity. This possibility is there particularly in the nature of the written law. That which can work through "the Law" is what is sometimes referred to as the "usurping Prince of this world." (See *The Inner Aspect of the Social Question*.)

Adverse Spiritual Powers

There is always the possibility of conflict leading to division in a community, when it is possible for a person, in a matter that is properly a concern of either cultural or economic life, to use the law or their rights to enforce their own will. We see one aspect of this in the extensive growth of litigation. In most cases it is where a person uses the force of law that gives them "rights" to gain monetary advantage out of what is "accident" or may indeed be the hand of destiny.

Let me give an example of the sort of thing that can happen in a school. This is an actual event that I have experienced. The details are changed, so that identities are protected.

I was once present at the Annual General Meeting of the Association of a school, that is of the legal body, made up of parents and teachers, that technically "owned" the school. I was not actively involved and was more of an observer. At this meeting each year they vote to pass the accounts, elect new members to the Board of the school to replace those retiring, and appoint the auditors. These actions were all required, and their form prescribed, by law.

In actual fact, it was a sort of annual rubber stamping in order to comply with the law. This group only met once a year - they really had no other purpose.

The school, that is the Board and the teachers, had decided to launch into a certain development which would incur considerable expenditure, and would use up certain existing funds. Some parents felt that the money should not be used for this purpose. They had tried hard to have the decision changed but without success. Those of this way of thinking on the Association then tried, as a means of enforcing their will, to get the annual general meeting to vote against passing the accounts.

The parent who felt most strongly about this and who was the main driving force behind the move to stop the development was someone who was and had been a long time and very active supporter of the school. There was no question but that she was committed to the education and stood behind the school. Her only concern was to help and support the school. But the whole tone of her voice and the tenor of what she said became antagonistic and destructive. It was actually out of character for this person to be like that. The same applied, though not so strongly, to the other parents who supported her. The experience was of a strong negative presence entering into the meeting.

What was happening was that a meeting set up to fulfill legal requirements and having a legal structure and form was being used to attempt to force a decision concerning educational and financial matters, that is whether money should go to this particular activity in the school that the teachers felt important. It was a situation that could clearly develop into a real destructive schism within the school.

Several people commented afterwards on how they experienced that something negative and destructive had entering into the meeting. This was something clearly not intended by those concerned, and not arising out of their own nature. It was such a strong experience that a group was formed to change the structure of the Association and to create another non-legal body where in future such questions could be heard and discussed without the legal presence.

This is just one but a particularly pronounced example of what I mean by adverse powers entering through the rights sphere. Most people who objectively observe meetings and the decision making process will have experienced something like this themselves. It is something that we must be awake to.

This again points to the necessity of learning to separate the three spheres of social life from each other and to work within each according to the laws appropriate to each.

The Rights Organ

It is important that there be an organ that carries responsibility for those affairs of the school that fall within the rights sphere. This organ will concern itself with all those matters that concern the school in that it has to conform to the requirements of the rights sphere of the locality in which it exists, with all the laws and regulations that govern the running of a school. It will also be responsible for the affairs that arise out of the rights life of the school community itself.

In order to comply with the legal requirements of the law of the country or state, there will of course already be a body, usually referred to as "the Board," the "Trustees," or the "Council." This has certain responsibilities defined by law, and often the school does not have a wide choice as to the way this is set up, but there is always some flexibility, usually more than people imagine. Later in this chapter I show how we at Emerson deal with this question. While for most schools it would not be possible or appropriate to copy this, it may give an idea how something could be attempted, but including parents and staff.

It is important that, however it is formed, the Board be sufficiently connected to the spiritual impulse out of which the school works, that the work it does and the decisions it makes will be true to that same spiritual impulse. This does not mean that everyone should be an anthroposophist. But it does mean there should be sufficient members who do work out of Anthroposophy, and others who, having chosen to bring their children to the school, are sufficiently committed to the impulse of the school to recognize its validity.

In my mind there are three things to which particular attention must be given in setting up the Board:

1) The Board should not be self perpetuating. The members ideally will be elected by a wider body comprised of both staff and parents of the school.

2) It is a mistake to think, as sometimes has happened, that the Board should consist mainly of people from "outside," who have expert knowledge in business, law, accounts, or such professions on the assumption that anthroposophists have no ability in these areas. Firstly,

this is not necessarily true, and secondly, this can divide the school into two parties, one looking outward and the other looking inward, with no common ground out of which both work. After a time they will each find they are working to a different purpose and from a different foundation. The Board then has legal control and can enforce its intentions on the school, even to getting rid of some teachers and appointing others. This is an extreme situation, but it has happened to a number of anthroposophical institutions, some of which can no longer be said to work out of Anthroposophy.

3) There should be as narrow a gap as possible between those who carry the impulse and the spiritual initiative in the school and those who are the "guardians of the law." This includes not only those who see that the school acts within the law, but also those who create the internal rights life of the school, who form the internal structures, rules, and agreements.

If internal structures, rules, and agreements are decided on by bodies such as the teachers meeting, then the teachers should take into account the fact that they are moving from the work of cultural life to that of rights life and adjust their thinking and approach accordingly.

Who Owns the School?

The question of who "owns" the school, who has the ultimate legal right to "hire and fire" people, to create or change policy or the aims of the school, is a very important one and must be given special attention. Modern law gives great power to those who own. It also establishes the difference in levels

163

between employer and employees. It does make a very great difference if people sense, even unconsciously, that they are employed by others who own the school, who have legal control over them, and who make the major decisions, or that it is their own work, that the circle of colleagues of which they are a member have control and run the school. It gives them a certain sense of freedom and of involvement, commitment and responsibility.

For reasons already given and to be further discussed, and from my own experience and observation, I am convinced that it is necessary as far as possible to overcome the separation between employer and employee, between those who own the school and those who carry the work. The people who carry the work of the school, that is the staff, should also own their work, be their own employers. This should be incorporated as far as possible into the legal framework of the school. A school will also have to consider how far this should also include parents, or some parents. Of course, this ownership should not give any financial or material benefits of any kind to those who do own the school.

Here again we have to relate and adapt to the laws and regulations of the particular country or state in which the school is established. Laws vary, both in space, that is from country to country, and in time, as new laws are enacted and come into force. Each school will have to decide the form and structure it wants to establish for itself, and then find the way to achieve this, or as near as possible, within the existing law.

Very often people too easily accept what they are told is possible within the law. It is not good in setting up a school to start from consideration of what the law allows. One should start by forming a picture of the form and structure needed in order to carry out the work intended and then to look to see how this can be achieved within the law. If one starts from a picture of the goal to be achieved and presents this, a good lawyer will nearly always be able to find a way of making it possible within the law. The law is never as rigid and all embracing as most people think.

But if it is not possible in law for those who work in such a school to also own it, it is often possible to create a situation where they are able to affect ownership in practice. This may be achieved through the working and decision making process between the staff and the Board and the way that Board is appointed.

But it is extremely important that the requirements of the law be understood and fulfilled. Failure to do so leaves open a door for all sorts of negative forces to enter and to divert, hinder, or destroy the intentions of the school.

Contracts of Employment

As mentioned above, when a new person joins the staff, there is a transformation from a free relationship to one bound by agreement or contract. But, as has been discussed, a person can only work out of their true impulses when they can do so in a situation of freedom, not one of compulsion through purchase or through the law. Great care must, therefore, be exercised that any contract does not extend beyond what is right and necessary and encroach into what should be a free situation.

The contract, whether verbal or written, can be seen and treated either as a reminder of what was agreed or as a commitment on either side enforceable by law. The extent to which it is enforceable will vary from one country to another.

It is also important that care be taken over the wording of any written agreement or contract. There is always the temptation to put more and more into an agreement. But it is better to put in no more than absolutely necessary to make clear the terms of the agreement. It is better that the agreement is seen as only there to make clear the basic arrangement in what is in reality a relationship of trust. It must be remembered that the more one relies on the written word the more it is possible to get caught in a conflict through the possibility of twisting the words to mean other than what was intended, and of one side to the agreement claiming to be bound by and responsible for only what is written. It is often just when there is tension and a breakdown in human relations that the written contract will be looked at with a certain intensity.

In many countries such a contract of employment is a requirement of the law, and the school must act responsibly according to the laws of the country of which it is a part. Here again there are two ways of going about this:

One is to start from what the law requires. This immediately puts one into a legalistic way of thinking. Such a way of thinking will tend to want to include clauses and requirements that go beyond what is strictly required by the law. The legal mind will tend to want to cover all eventualities, and so one begins to go down the slippery slope. It will result in a contract that may well be good from the point of view of the law, but will not in anyway reflect the way of working that is fundamental to a Waldorf school.

Or one can start from what the school itself feels is necessary and reflects the spirit out of which it works. This should start from what was the actual basis of the invitation to the individual to work in the school. Ideally, the contract should be a memorandum of the decisions arrived at in conversation, a reminder of what was agreed, not itself the agreement. Having arrived at a form of words that is true to the spiritual foundation of the school, then one looks to see what the law requires and incorporates this into it.

There is something else, to take further what was said in Chapter Four. It is in the nature of the sphere of rights that whenever there are rules or laws, particularly if these are in written form, then the focus of a person's will is to act within the law, according to the meaning of the written word, rather than to act out of one's own sense of what is right action. For example, in a job description or a contract of employment, the more detail that is included the more both parties will be bound by what is actually written and by only that. The more detail that is included, the greater the tendency to act only according to the written word and to put aside individual responsibility and initiative.

For example, it may be stated as part of the contract that a person will teach 20 hours per week. Time, which is measurable, can be put into the contract, but the quality of the teaching, which cannot be so measured, is not then included. The focus of consciousness of the teacher and of the school will then be on the time, on the measurable, that the teacher works rather than on the nature of that teaching.

One might think that this would not apply to people working out of Anthroposophy. But that is not so. There is a particular danger, just when such organizations come out of the pioneer stage and people want to get away from the hassle of dealing with all the idiosyncrasies of other people's behavior. Then it seems easier to have rules which must be followed. Anthroposophists can on occasion be just as impatient with each other as others are.

There is a story about Rudolf Steiner. (One does wonder how many of these stories are true, but it does make an important point.) He was asked why so often nice people, when they become anthroposophists, then become selfish and unsociable. He replied that one should imagine a house that has not been lived in for a long time, that has lain dormant for many years; what happens when someone moves in to live there? First, she has to get to work with the broom and the duster, and then the dirt and the dust begin to fly.

The Structure of Emerson College

I will give here, by way of illustration, some aspects of the way Emerson College is formed and works. I am fully aware that in England and in most other countries it may not now be possible to structure a college or school in just such a way. Emerson, in its present form, was established under the laws as they were in 1967 in this country.

Despite this, I do believe there is value in looking at the way the College has come to work. To see how others have found ways of working together out of the recognition of the three spheres of social life must always be helpful. Even if they cannot be copied, they can help to generate new ideas. That they cannot just be copied can even be an advantage, as every institution has to find its own form, which must take into account the particular people involved, the place, and its stage of development. Because a particular structure is right for one institution does not mean it is right for others, or even for itself at a different time. There must always be development and growth, which involves change. An institution, such as a school, is a living organism, and life means change and development.

I should add that, as the College developed and grew out of the pioneer stage, we have constantly adjusted and modified the way we work, but the basic structure has remained much the same. The experience that I draw on is from the time I was bursar. I have now retired and am no longer involved on the various central bodies of the College, so I cannot say this is exactly how things are still; there have been changes, but I do believe the basic form is still maintained.

I must also say that I will tend to give the ideal that we have striven for. We are all human; there have been many ups and downs, and we have frequently not lived up to or fully achieved our ideals. But I do believe that the way we work together has been part of the strength of the College, in that it has enabled and encouraged all members of staff to give something extra of the best that lives in them.

As far as anyone owns Emerson College, it is owned by the people who work there. Being a charity, or a not-for-profit company, the "owners" cannot in any way benefit financially from this ownership, so some of the problems that can arise from "ownership" are overcome. But it does make a great difference for those who carry the work to feel, "This is my work; I am not employed by others, by a body that is quite separate from me. I am not controlled through ownership. We are the employers of ourselves." It generates a sense of freedom, colleagueship, and mutual responsibility.

When a person has been at the College for about a year, perhaps longer in the case of part time work, and is here on an ongoing commitment, and provided she herself can say that she works out of Anthroposophy, then she will normally be invited to apply to become a member of what we call the Association, but more correctly The Emerson College Trust Ltd. For this purpose the actual work she does is immaterial. Her application for membership is then accepted (or not) by the council of management. She will remain a member until she leaves the College. People who do not work at the College can also be appointed as members for three years at a time.

The members, as members, meet once a year at the Annual General Meeting for the purpose of fulfilling certain legal requirements. One is to elect the council of management, something like the shareholders of a company electing the board of directors.

This council meets every week, and sometimes on a weekend. It normally consists of about ten people whose main work is at the College. It fulfills the functions and responsibilities that the Board or Trustees do in other institutions, that is, the carrying of the legal responsibility for the College activities and financial affairs.

In addition, the council is the main decision making body within the College for all matters other than pedagogical questions, which are the responsibility of the faculty meeting. But even then, if the faculty failed to fulfill its task or fell apart, it would be the council that would be ultimately responsible. It makes the final decision as to taking on new members of staff, and on new developments, initiatives, and policy. It has to mediate between the financial possibilities and the needs of the work. It is also responsible for the maintenance and development of the buildings and environment. To achieve all this it can and does appoint committees, including a management committee.

All council members are expected to attend the staff meeting and also the faculty meeting, even if they are not themselves teachers. This is important. If the council, for example, has to make the final decision as to whether a particular initiative goes ahead, it is greatly helped to do this in a spiritually healthy way, if the members are also in those meetings where they can develop a sense for what lives as "will" in other members of the College. It is not that they can necessarily contribute to a discussion within the faculty, but they may later have to make a decision, for instance concerning money, or the structure of the College, that could hinder or support what the teachers see as important. It is so easy for those in authority, especially when they control the money supply, to kill impulses and initiatives that spring from individuals, or which arise out of what lives as future work in, for example, the faculty meeting. Only out of direct experience with the initiators of an impulse can they know that impulse and bring a proper balance between the money and that which "wills to come about."

Only members of the Association can be elected members of the council and the number can vary but is normally about ten. One third of the members must retire each year at the annual general meeting, but they can stand for re-election together with any other nominations. That is the legal requirement.

But only part of the work of the council comes within the sphere of rights. The main work of the College lies within cultural life, and so much of the work of the council also lies there. It is also responsible for the economic affairs of the College. A normal democratic election of council members is, therefore, not appropriate. The way we do this is an example of how the law can be fulfilled in a way that also fulfills the needs of the College.

One member of the council, who is not due to retire, is asked to form an election committee. She asks two members of the Association who are not on the council, and who are not hoping to stand for election themselves, to join her and so form a committee of three.

This committee then has discussions with the council and also brings the subject of the membership of the council to the staff meeting for discussion. The work and task of the council, future questions, and work to be tackled during the coming year, and criteria for membership are the sort of matters that would be looked at. It is generally agreed that each year there should be some change in membership, and that there should be on the council a consciousness of the whole College, although no one "represents" their own area of work. The different sexes and temperaments bring different capacities, which are all needed for the healthy working of the council and must be included. It is also felt that consideration should be given to including young members who have come into their work and are ready to take on wider responsibility. After this meeting with the staff there is a week or so for any colleagues to individually put in suggestions or proposals to the committee.

The members of the committee then consider what they have heard and come forward with a proposal as to who should be elected or re-elected to the council for the coming year. Their proposal has always been accepted and has then gone through as a formality at the Annual General Meeting.

This way means that everyone can have their say and be heard as to the membership of that body that carries ultimate responsibility for the impulse of the College and that "makes the rules." Also, it means that most people who work full time at the college at some time have been or will be themselves on the council and so at the center of the decision making.

Employer / Employee

One thing that is achieved by this is that it gives substance to the intention that everyone is a colleague, a co-carrier, not an employee. It also gives expression to the recognition that in this sphere each member of staff is seen as equal to all others. Of course, legally we are employees, but as members of the Association we are in a sense also the employers. We as a circle are the college. This also means that there is not a wide separation between each member of staff and "the council." "They" are "us." The whole works as a unity.

Chapter Fourteen

Salaries and Fees / Rights Life

The questions of both salaries and tuition fees or contributions bridges the rights and economic spheres. Basically, we can say that the way salaries are paid, the basis on which the amounts are arrived at, not the actual amounts, is a matter that must arise out of the general feeling, the common opinion of the whole community, where everyone's opinion is of equal value. But the practical details of the actual amounts to be contributed by the parents and to be paid to staff is a responsibility of the economic sphere. That will be considered in Chapters Eighteen and Nineteen.

We can study the nature of payment and of salaries or of tuition fees in great depth. We can come to the recognition that labor cannot be bought, that education is not an economic product, and that the teacher's salary is a gift. We can come to an understanding of all this. But in the actual life of a school or other such organization, it will be out of the feeling life of those involved that the system of calculating salaries will be seen as fair and just or as unfair and inequitable. Of course, these feelings will be influenced and changed when a perception of the true nature of economics and of the threefold nature of social life is nurtured in the community. But these feelings as they are must be given space to express themselves in the rights sphere of the school.

Whatever the leaders, the wise heads or the board may know is a right or "anthroposophical" way of calculating and charging fees and paying salaries, if parents or staff feel it to be unfair, it will cause social unrest and division. These feelings can be informed and educated, but here it is the feelings of all those affected that must be the guide, not the knowledge and understanding of the few. In this every person must be given an equal say in the decision.

Salaries

In the world at large today it is widely accepted that people are paid for their work, and that there should be no discrimination. The salary they receive must be based on the work, or the product of the work, and all must be treated equally in this; only this is considered to be fair. Here too often there is a confusion between "equal" and "same." Many feel that to pay a person according to her needs or her personal circumstances, rather than for her work, is inequitable. "Equal pay for equal work" is understood as "the same pay for the same work."

Many, perhaps most, people who come to work in an anthroposophical institution bring these thoughts and feelings with them as accepted wisdom. Although they may question conventional education, medicine, methods of food production, and much else, they feel a certain security in conventional thinking when it comes to the money they receive as salary and on which they live.

Whatever the rights or wrongs of conventional thinking or of the economics as outlined in this book, the feelings that arise out of the one or the other in individuals are actual and real and have social consequences. They must be listened to. In this sense feelings are not right or wrong; they exist and must form the basis of rights life.

Feelings cannot be changed at will. Change can only be brought about gradually through study and observation of the actual realities of life, of money and the threefold nature of social life, and through the awakening to the true being of every person one meets. Then the feelings will be transformed and will come to be based on what is true, rather than on illusion. Through these transformed feelings will come the will to work and live in a way that is true to our time and to the Spirit. Only when the feelings towards money and each other have changed in sufficient numbers of the staff, and the will arises for a new way of forming their community, can the necessary changes be realized in practice.

A community that does not take into account the feelings of its members, irrespective of the nature of those feelings, will find antisocial forces entering into the community, which will work destructively. This is particularly true where it concerns money. Money always has the tendency to awaken feelings that are antisocial and destructive.

Another aspect of the nature of rights life and of salaries is one many people have probably themselves experienced in some form. It is one that needs to be understood, particularly in its manifestation in the particular school. It is this:

Many schools and other such organizations were originally founded when a few people came together out of a common intention to found the school, or to actively work with and support someone who was doing so. They were the pioneers. In such a pioneer situation it is usually the case that there is not enough money, and so from the beginning they do not receive what might be considered adequate salaries. In fact, very often they go without much of what is generally considered essential to a reasonable life. But their impulse to get the school going is so strong that they will forgo much in order to achieve what they have set out to do.

There arises an unspoken common opinion of a minimum standard of living that they all sense and abide by in order to achieve the work they have set themselves.

Over time, and as the school develops, this "common opinion," or accepted common standard of living, begins to rise. New people joining the original group will sense it and adjust to it. But the older the school the longer new comers will take to find this common standard. I experienced this often at Emerson. Later in the life of the school new people will come who have great difficulty in sensing the common standard. Eventually it will have to be formalized. What was unconscious, what lived in a group as a common opinion, has to be made conscious.

Where people earlier were able to go without many things, they begin to find this difficult or even impossible. They will need a high level of salary. However salaries are paid, some may come to feel that they are unreasonable.

That which rises as "common opinion" is the basis of the rights life. In a small group it can often be almost unspoken; people just know it or sense it. But later it has to be discussed, agreed, and formalized. Perhaps it will have to be put into writing. This happens with many aspects of the community life other than salaries.

Needs Based?

Probably one of the most important decisions the staff will have to make out of the rights sphere is the question of how salaries should be paid, whether on a conventional basis, that is on a scale relative to qualifications and nature of work, on a scale relative to needs, or on a free individual needs basis. The details, merits, and importance of a needs based salary system will be considered in more detail in the next three chapters.

At Emerson we have worked on a form of individual needs based salary ever since the College was founded in 1962. It will be illustrative to give something of the way we give this validity through the support of the whole staff.

As far as I can remember, there have been three main occasions when we have reviewed the way we dealt with salaries in the staff meeting. The main questions that came up were:

1) Do we continue as we are, or move towards some sort of salary scale? This has been a question that has been discussed in the whole staff meeting on several occasions over the last 25 years or so. It has always eventually been agreed to continue with the unscaled needs based salary. Although on each occasion there were one or two who felt differently, they did say that they felt their opinion had been listened to, and they were happy to go with the majority decision.

2) What level of need do we support? This is always a difficult question. It has to arise out of the feelings of all the colleagues and of what is financially available as a totality. People

can to a very great extent adjust their needs to what is available only if they experience that they are a part of the whole and are fully carried and informed of what is happening and why. Also, only to the extent that they feel this is their work and that they are one with the work and purpose of the college or school will they be able to adjust their needs to a level that is sustainable and compatible with the healthy continuation of that work.

3) Do we all know what each person receives? We have always come to the agreement that we do not want to do so. For me to know what another person needs or receives is only justified if I also know why she needs it. To do that I must know a great deal about her, including something of her karma. To know what she feels she needs without an objective understanding of why she feels she needs it is opening a Pandora's box of misunderstandings, suspicions, false judgments, and other socially destructive emotions. To fully know why each of some thirty or forty people need what they do would take considerable time, study, and energy. Our work is primarily to work with students, not on each other. We have always felt this task should be left to a small group in whom the rest have confidence.

4) What form of salary committee should we have and how is its membership to be arrived at? We have come to several different answers here. The most interesting one was when each of us wrote on a piece of paper the names of four colleagues with whom we would be comfortable talking about our needs. Out of these lists we were able to find three to form a salary group which contained at least one person from each list. If a person wanted to talk over her needs, she did not have to meet the whole group, but could do it with the person she could relate to.

What I have discussed here is how the basic form must first be given to salaries by the rights life within the school. It is one that too often is not given the attention needed.

I have tried to show that the question of salaries or wages bridges the rights and economic spheres. Fundamentally, we can say that the basis on which salaries are paid, the method by which the amounts are arrived at, is a matter that must arise out of the general feeling, the common opinion of the whole community, where everyone's opinion is of equal value. But the actual amounts that each receives, the individual needs of each person, and also the calculation of how much to charge parents and how much of this goes to salaries and to other needs of the school, such as maintenance of buildings and insurance, are the responsibility of the economic sphere. The two spheres here are intimately connected and work together and must work also with cultural life. It is not possible to divide the question of salaries into two clearly defined sections, one rights and one economic. What is important is that at any one place we can see the influences, the laws at work that come from the different directions. I hope this will become clearer as we look more deeply into the subject.

Tuition Fees or Contributions

In a school the relationship of the standard of living of the parents and that of the staff is also a factor that must be worked with. Can a working together and a common imagination be so built within the whole body of staff and parents that all feel it fair that the standard of living should find some sort of balance on both sides? This will, of course, be difficult, as it is extremely unlikely that there is any common standard within the parent body. There will be parents who are poor and others who are better off.

I felt it to be fair and equitable – that the staff, who teach the children of the parents, have a standard of living below the average parent, equal to, or above it? Such a question will raise many others that could be discussed. Is it acceptable that poor parents have to enable the teacher of their child to live at a standard above their own, or should the wealthy pay so little that the teacher has to live well below their own lifestyle? The task here is to arrive, not at what each wants, not at how much can one receive, and how little can the other pay, but at developing the feeling on both sides of something being fair and equitable to both.

Much of what has been said above about salaries applies also to the question of tuition fees or contributions paid by the parents. There is a general assumption that salaries should and do vary between different people, even if only due to such factors as the nature of the work or the qualifications of the teacher. But there is no such general assumption that there should be different fees for different parents. On the contrary, there is a strong presumption that all should pay the same. Although there might be different fees for lower and higher classes, this is the same for all parents.

It is just this question as to whether every parent should pay or contribute the same amount, or if not, how to arrive at just and fair amounts, that is a question for the rights sphere. Present thinking on this question arises out of the general assumption that it is a question of economic purchase.

To get people to see that there may be other ways of looking at "tuition fees" is probably more difficult than getting staff to move to other ways of paying "salaries." In the parent body there is often a wide spread group of people, from those with a deep and committed connection to Anthroposophy to others with no interest at all, who see no more than that it seems to be the best education available in their area for their children.

But my experience is that we underestimate what will interest parents and what they will understand. We must get away from a moralistic or patronizing approach. More parents than we might imagine will understand what is said in the next chapter, both that which arises out of the purely economic factors, and that which arises out of an observation of life itself. But we must first come to see the truth of these things for ourselves. Only when we speak out of what we ourselves know to be true will a real interest be awakened in others. Then parents will come to want other ways of dealing with the question of the parent financial support for the school, because they will come to feel that the present system is neither efficient nor equitable. Then, also, can the will be fired.

I do believe that many parents with little connection with Anthroposophy will actually understand these things more directly than many anthroposophists themselves. They will recognize from their experience in life itself the truth of what is said.

I will look into tuition fees or contributions in Chapters Eighteen and Nineteen.

Chapter Fifteen

Economic - Salaries

The two most important aspects of money in a school and the two that, in my experience, raise more questions than anything else are tuition fees and staff salaries. First, I will look at salaries, and then, in the following two chapters I will discuss fees.

What I bring here is not based on any moral ethic, but on the demands of the inherent nature and actual laws of the three-fold social structure and money. These are in themselves moral, and we have to learn to act accordingly.

The salary a person receives can be a very personal thing and often touches the feelings and emotions very deeply. Many people experience in their salary a measure of their worth or of how others judge their worth. They can also experience it as the price for which they sell something of themselves, their labor. On the one level it can be felt as that for which a person has to sacrifice her freedom, an enslavement, or at the opposite extreme the goal for which she works, that which contains a promise of freedom and even of a kind of utopia.

The way salaries are worked with in an organization can cause considerable feelings of injustice, discrimination, and resentment. In the same organization there are nearly always some who can easily manage on their salary and others who suffer considerable hardship, even though they are "colleagues" carrying the same work. The approach to salaries can make it possible for a person to put their whole life and work into the school, or just so much as is needed to earn their salary. The way the salary is calculated can effect what a person feels she needs.

To a large extent the whole sphere of salaries functions in the hidden depths of the school. The basis of the education and the activities in the classrooms with the children, the relationships to the parents, their problems, and the questions of fees are all more present, open and often discussed than the questions of salaries. In many institutions it is hardly mentioned. Conventional methods are used, and they continue to function with a kind of inevitability. All the feelings and emotions that arise remain in the hidden depths.

We need to look carefully at our salary arrangements and bring them out into the light of day. Are they derived from old concepts, ones that were relevant to an earlier human consciousness and social configuration, or can we say that they are appropriate to the human being of today and to that towards which evolution is unfolding into the future?

Are our salary arrangements based on true reality, or are they based on untruths, on illusion?

These are important questions and touch matters that can affect the whole social culture and well being of a school. Outside of all that relates to the actual teaching, salaries are probably the single most important and far reaching question.

Payment for Work or Contribution towards Needs

As we have seen, in order for the school and staff to exist and do their work, they depend for the basic physical necessities of life almost wholly on the economic activities of the wider community, not the immediate community but the wider world community. What the school receives by way of money as fees, gifts, or taxes, and what is paid as salaries enables the staff to obtain the products of those who work in economic production. Most schools produce nothing or very little by way of actual economic products for themselves, except for example, where they provide housing and meals or run a shop. They are, in the main, and so far as the economic sphere is concerned, pure consumers. Their only actual economic activity is as consumers. The money gives them the power or authority to draw on the productivity of the community.

It must always be remembered that it is the products of other people's labor on which the school and its staff live, not on the money. Through this the school is connected quite directly to the world community. We are here looking at the social and financial life of the school, not from the basis of any modern economic theories or established thought forms that are in use today, but from an observation of realities, which is what Rudolf Steiner pointed to.

Generally today, and within most anthroposophical institutions, the basis on which salaries and wages are calculated is one or more of the following:

1) The work the person does. Work or labor is treated as a commodity that is purchased like any other input to a factory or economic productive activity. The worker sells her labor. Teaching is also a commodity and is purchased by the employer. Many schools may throw up their collective hands in horror at the idea that they work in this way, but if they looked carefully at the foundation of the thinking behind their salaries, they would see that this is not far off the mark.

2) The market price for the job. This is a refinement of #1 in that it establishes the price for the job on purely market forces.

3) The earning or value creating power of the person. This is based on the extra business and increase in profit that will be generated by this individual's activity and expertise. It is a development of #2. The remuneration of top management and financial advisors is usually based on this. But it omits the fact that such a person is always part of a team, and such profits would not be generated if many others were not also there.

4) The qualifications the person has attained. Here again we are putting a price on the person herself. A qualified person is of more value than one not so qualified. The human individual is being valued on economic criteria, like a product or a machine.

5) The length of time the person takes to do the work. Here it is the time which has a price, but it is really no different from the pricing of the work itself. We can no more buy a person's time than we can her labor. Here we have a picture of a person having so many hours or days of life, and she sells some of these to earn money on which to live. But this again is an unreality. In actual fact, in economic life, it is the product of the work she does during that time that is exchanged for money and which enables her in turn to receive the products of other people's work.

Ultimately the pay is related to the nature of the work itself, not the individual person who works. It is calculated on the productivity or quality of the work, the time worked, the value of the work, or a combination of these. It is seen as fair when people doing the same work receive the same pay. When it is seen thus, it must follow that it is understood as a purchase of the work.

In many schools a person is expected to work a given number of hours. If she works less, she will be paid less. If she is not paid less, then feelings can emerge amongst her colleagues that she is "not earning her salary." If she works more, then feelings can arise in her based on the thought that she is either not being paid for the work she does or that she is "making a gift of her work."

Where there are increments according to qualifications, this must be based on the recognition that either the quality of the work itself is better, or the results, the education of the children, will be better. In both cases it is based on the idea that it is the work that is being paid for, that is purchased.

In all the above situations we are treating either the work or the result of the work as something that can be bought or sold; we are thinking in terms of the economic productive process, not of the free human being. To think in any of these ways, to treat a person or their work as an economic product that can be bought and sold denies something of the truly human in a person. This will have its consequences.

We talk about "paying for the work," "the cost of labor," and "the labor market." What do these mean? Do such statements make sense? Do we pay "for work"? Can we buy work? We saw earlier that in economic life this is nonsense; we only exchange or buy the products of work. Work itself is not a product that can be given "in exchange."

Work is what a person does; it is human activity. A person's work, whether it is for herself or for others, is a part of herself; it is not something separate. Life itself or being alive is an activity. Without something to do, without work, we would be vegetables. When we pay for or buy someone's work, we are buying something that is an essential aspect, an integral part of their being. Although to buy labor is in actual reality an impossibility, when we think and act as though it has reality, then there will be disruptive social consequences.

We have also seen in Chapter Seven that irrespective of the way the money comes to the school, whether as fees, gifts, or tax money from the state, within the proper life cycle of money it has the nature of gift money. Somehow or other this money arises as surplus within the economic sphere of social activity and has to be passed as gift to cultural life, there to purchase what would otherwise be the excess products of economic production. We saw from various different perspectives that money, depending on where it is within the cycle, has different values and qualities. Gift money provides the possibility of freeing the human being, of bringing into life those intuitions that arise within the creative thinking human being. In the school it has the capacity to free the teacher to teach, and through this to nurture the potential capacities and resolves that the child brings from pre-birth existence.

We saw in Chapter Three with the example of the baker and the lecturer that what the teacher receives as salary is not the price of a purchase. There is no economic product nor any exchange of products in education or other such cultural life activity. Value arises in economic life through division-of-labor. But division-of-labor plays no part, and no such economic value arises in cultural life. There a person teaches, in so far as she is rightfully doing so, because her karma placed her there in order to fulfill her pre-birth resolves. In teaching she is fulfilling the demands of her own destiny, as well as assisting in the destiny of her pupils. It is extremely important that this be perceived as true, otherwise what is said in this book will have no foundation.

In actual reality, the pay that the teacher or other cultural workers receive is of the nature of gift. It enables her to obtain that which she needs of the products of economic life. It frees her from having herself to join in the economic production process.

The question then arises, if her salary is not a purchase, if it cannot be calculated on the work itself, nor on the product of the work, on what basis do we calculate how much she is given?

I have shown above that we cannot calculate this on the actual work she does. If we do, we may then think we are giving her the money, that we are freeing her, but we will not be doing so. If we calculate what she is paid in any way on the work she does, then we are paying for her work, and we are not freeing her to do the work.

If we pay a person in order to free her to work, we can only do this on the basis of calculating what she needs, that is, on what she needs in order to be free to teach, not on the basis of the work itself. The experience of the human soul in the one or the other case is fundamentally different, and the importance of this difference should not be underestimated.

One person may need only a small amount. Another in different circumstances may need a much greater amount to fulfill her family or other responsibilities. Some people will then say that it is not fair to give one person more than another, although they do the same work. But this argument can only be valid, if we base it on the work rather than the person. We then come back to paying for the work. But if one person has children who depend on her for their needs, and another has no dependents, is it "fair" that they each get the same, or that the one gets enough for the children as well as herself, whereas the other gets enough for herself? Or again, one may be born with a karma that means she has a need to travel and to see different parts of the world in order for her to make her contribution to humanity, while another does not have that need. Perhaps her need is one that does not require the same income to be fulfilled. Is it then unfair to apportion what is available according to what each needs to fulfill her life?

When we talk of paying people on a basis of need, this does not mean that we meet a person's every need. It means that the calculation of what a person is to receive is based on what she needs rather than on the work she does. In this everyone is treated equally. If there is not enough to meet everyone's perceived needs, then everyone will have to reduce their needs proportionately, or receive an equal proportion of their total needs.

It will not be easy to free ourselves from the domination of the present way of thinking - that we pay for work, that we buy a person's labor. But before we can change the way we pay ourselves, we must change our thinking.

Chapter Sixteen

Salaries - Needs Based as a Necessity of Human Evolution

Many people do question whether it really is important or necessary to move away from a tried, straight forward, and generally accepted way of paying people to one that must be riddled with problems, and appears to originate more from sentiment and new age thinking than from any real perception of economic and social factors. There are also those who argue that ideas of needs based salaries are illusory and not something arrived at from a real understanding of Anthroposophy and of the threefold social order.

We are touching something here that is a more profound question of our time than many seem to realize. It is one that has relevance for the whole of humanity, not just for Waldorf schools. But it is one not easy to fathom. Rudolf Steiner, as so often was his way, did not spell it out in detail, but he did frequently point to it from various directions.

For instance, in the sixth lecture, given on July 29, 1922, of the series translated as *World Economy*, he gave a kind of formula for the "true price" of an economic product. What he said is translated as:

"A true price is forthcoming when a person receives, as counter-value for the products he has made, sufficient to enable him to satisfy the whole of his needs, including those of his dependents, until he will have made another like product.

Abstract as it is, this formula is none the less exhaustive. In setting up a formula it is always necessary that it should contain all the concrete details. I do believe, for the domain of economics, this formula is no less exhaustive than, say, the theorem of Pythagoras is for all right-angled triangles."

This is not the place to go into all that arises out of this statement except to say that it talks quite specifically of "needs," including those of dependents, and relates to future needs, not those of the past. Here he is speaking more directly about economics, but if this is true for that sphere, it cannot be less so for the cultural life. But there it cannot be "as counter value for the products he has made." He says much the same thing in his book originally published in English as *The Threefold Commonwealth* and more recently as *Towards Social Renewal*.

Also, in other lectures on different subjects he pointed to this demand coming out of the evolutionary impulses working in humanity, that is, that the individual human being is made free and not tied to economic forces of sale and purchase.

I am going into this question of needs based salary at some length, because I do believe:

1) that there is considerable confusion at present in anthroposophical circles, and some quite misleading statements and claims have been made concerning it;

2) it is an integral component of the threefold social life. There can be no real freedom for the individual in the cultural sphere, unless there is also that which gives it possibility in the economic sphere; and it is so fundamentally a part of the whole that without it there can be no real grasp of the interrelationships and interweaving within the threefold social life and of its wisdom filled nature.

3) it is a demand of the evolutionary forces of our time and already experienced in the subconscious depths of the human soul.

I hope there are people who will take up some of these aspects for further study and research. If teachers of Waldorf schools take seriously, as I know many do, the necessity to work also out of the needs of the world and of the humanity of our time, then this question cannot be ignored.

I have already gone some way to looking at it from the perspective of economic life. I would like briefly to touch on some further points.

The Balance to the Egoism of Cultural Life

We should look at something else that comes from quite a different direction but which points to the same necessity. It is something which will grow ever more important as humanity crosses the threshold, and the three soul capacities of thinking, feeling , and willing become separated.

We saw earlier that in cultural life there is always an element of egoism, not in a negative sense, but in that a person works and creates out of her own inner need, out of that which she longs to be or to accomplish. This egoism has its rightful place; without it there would be no cultural life, no development of the human soul. But there must be something in society as a whole that brings it into balance, that resolves the adverse consequences of this egoism.

For this we must look at economic life. (But economic thinking has, of course, spread into the rest of social life, so to that extent what I say applies to all "wages.") If in the economic sphere a person is paid for her work, she must see her work as that for which she is paid. The more or better her work the more her value, the higher her salary. It is clear from an observation of life that this inevitably leads to the thought, "I am a value and I must be paid for my value, for my productive value." So her thoughts are turned inwards to herself and what is due to her rather than outwards as how to produce what it is that people need. Then there develops alongside the one necessary egoism in the cultural life a second egoism in economic life. This cannot balance or counter the first. On the contrary, egoism in the economic sphere will only strengthen the negative effects of that which has its proper place in the cultural sphere. Social life will be permeated by egoism instead of by a balance, a breathing between egoism and altruism.

We saw that division-of-labor in economic production actually demands mutuality, altruism. We also saw that the excess capital which arises in economic life, as a result of the creative imaginations coming from cultural life, must be given over to cultural life. We saw that this is an economic necessity. It is this mutuality, this giving from economic life that must be there to counter balance the egoism of cultural life. This is achieved when the money the cultural worker receives as salary is a gift. Only then is economic life made healthy and the teacher free.

The working in balance of these two poles, egoism and mutuality or free gift, is as essential to community as breathing in and breathing out are to life.

People who have always been paid on the basis of payment for work may well think that it will not really make such a difference, or be of benefit, to pay according to need, especially with all the difficulties that one imagines this might create. But we have all experienced being in a situation where there is a constant back ground noise, such as a pump or fan. After a while we get use to and cease to be aware of it - until it stops. Then there is sudden relief. Only then do we become conscious of the pressure we have been under. So it can be with changing from payment for work to giving on a basis of need.

Can the Future Live in the Teacher?

We can then ask, is this something demanded by the evolutionary impulses of our time, and what does it mean for Waldorf schools?

The teacher has to understand something of the journey of the souls of the children, that they have come through earlier earth lives and from worlds of Spirit. She must also develop a prophetic sense of what will come in the future, of the nature of the future the children are facing. There will already live in many of the souls before her a question as to the tasks of the future and a resolve to work towards that which has to come about.

What is necessary is that the incarnating soul be surrounded by teachers in whom there lives at least some understanding for, and a striving to work out of, the evolutionary forces of our time active in the world. If such a conscious aim and purpose does not permeate the spiritual environment of the Waldorf school, where do those souls go to who as children must find in their teachers that which can give them a true picture of the world into which they have been born, and in which lies their future work? As the teacher must know, a great deal of that which the child learns, but which only blossoms later in adulthood, comes not from what is directly taught but from what lives in the souls of the adults that surround her in childhood.

The way salaries are handled in a school must not be a matter only of administrative convenience, or to develop a social harmony amongst the teachers. It must come about that the human being is made free and independent in every respect, that pay can only be on a basis of need and not on the amount or quality of work or time. The children, in the depths of their souls, will know if the teachers also live and act out of those truths that are the basis of the education.

From Slavery to Freedom

Can we come to know the evolutionary impulses of our age? In earlier times in a certain sense human beings were bought and sold - that was slavery. The Greek culture in all its greatness flourished on an economy based on slavery. It could not have been otherwise. At that time there was even a certain justification for it. That was before the time of the consciousness soul. Human beings still lived in a kind of group soul consciousness. The individual did not have a separate consciousness and being as she does today.

Then the whole human being was bought and sold, not just her labor. One human being was owned by another. Later came a certain freeing when the serf, the vassal, or other form of bonded servant emerged. One human being did not own the whole of another; ownership was limited but still present.

But we now live in the time of the Consciousness or Spiritual Soul, of the awakening of the individual Ego. The human being struggles to be free, to be individual and herself, not part of a group soul. But our social life perpetuates the old forms. It has not found those that are appropriate for the new age. We still buy a part of the human being, her activity, her work. When we pay for work, when we buy labor, we are continuing that which started as slavery. When a person experiences her work as being bought, she feels it in conflict with that which wells up from the unconscious depths of her being, the demand to be an individual and free human being. During the time that she is bought, she is not herself. Then she creates an artificial division between herself and her work.

There is then the tendency to take no responsibility for the work she does, and she sleeps through it or rebels against the system. Something of the individual human being dies, and she becomes a sort of clone of the organization for which she works. Today we see this more and more in the life of institutions and businesses. Of course, it manifests differently in different people and in different situations, but that which is a demand of our time is always there in the depths of the human soul.

When in our institutions and communities we still pay people for their work, we are in conflict with the demands of our time and of what must come in the future, and also with economic reality. It will become ever more urgent that humanity finally abandon what belongs to the past, what is a remnant of the old slavery. A new way must be found of paying people, of giving them their share of the produce of an economy that is now a communal mutual activity. We have to find a way that leaves the individual free. It is a demand of our time.

A Demand of Evolution

Another demand of the evolutionary forces working in our time is the "Threefold Social Order" itself. Rudolf Steiner indicates this in several places.

At the laying of the foundation stone of the first Goetheanum on September 20, 1913, he gave a brief but significant address. During this he twice spoke the words, which he gave then for the first time, of what is known as the Macrocosmic Lord's Prayer. During the following year he gave in different places a number of courses of lectures on *The Fifth Gospel*. In each of the three courses that have been translated into English, those given in Oslo, Berlin, and Cologne, he spoke of the Macrocosmic Lord's Prayer, and of how this prayer of ancient times, the prayer of humanity's decent into Earth existence, was given to Jesus of Nazareth before the baptism in the Jordan. He speaks of all that led up to the transformation of this Macrocosmic Lord's Prayer into the Microcosmic Lord's Prayer that was given by Christ Jesus, the prayer to enable humanity to find its way back again to the worlds of Spirit.

Study all that he brought again and again in each of these lectures, look at the particular sufferings of Jesus of Nazareth, of the deep questions that arose in his experience at the gates of the Essenes. Look at the deep and painful questions that arose in him concerning those who had to labor, the "publicans and sinners," those who were exposed to Ahriman and Lucifer by the nature of having to work to earn the money with which to buy "bread," and how it was out of this that the Lord's Prayer as we have it today was given. Look also at all that is signified by the temptation of Christ to "turn stones into bread." Then look into what lies in the middle lines of the two prayers, those concerning the "daily bread."

If we do all this, if we then place it into the course of human evolution as given by Spiritual Science, and into the unfolding of division-of-labor as the foundation of economic life, we will be led again and again to the threefold social life of humanity and to the necessity of separating work from money.

Study the lectures on *World Economy* given by Rudolf Steiner and also the three he gave in Oxford in August, 1922.

If we do all this, we will come to a clear recognition of the demand of human evolution, as it will continue to unfold in the future: that the human being is finally freed from herself being a part of the process of economic production. Then no part of her, her work, or of that which arises out of her individual creative and imaginative capacities will be bought or sold. The free and individual human being will stand outside the economic process of production. This will function as a separate process operating as a result of her work and creative capacities, but not incorporating them.

Then we will see also that the only possible basis for salaries or wages in the future will be one that is of the nature of gift and is related to the needs of the individual.

This is looking at what wills to come about in the future. Perhaps it can be realized only in the distant future. But the need for it is already present. It is felt by many in the world at large. Observe and listen to the demands of the trade unions and their members. Listen also to the questions of management, to people in the professions. Observe how people are trying out new ideas, how many rebel against what arises as payment for work. This

199

is only faintly there, but it can be heard through keen and patient observation; it is already emerging as an impulse of our time. If we do this we will see that dimly, just below the level of consciousness, there is a growing demand that wages be calculated differently from the way they are now.

Chapter Seventeen

Salaries - Needs Based

Having emphasized the importance of needs based salaries, I must now emphasize that any school thinking of moving towards setting one up must think very carefully before embarking on such a major change. It is comparatively easy to move from needs based to conventional salaries. It is much more difficult to move in the opposite direction. To move in the one direction has an element of being allowed to go to sleep, in the other of having to wake up.

In my opinion any attempt to convert to a needs based salary system without careful preparation will only lead to disaster. To start with, it is essential that all three spheres are worked on together, not just salaries in isolation. They each provide the necessary supports and balances to the others.

Although, to a certain extent, every school is different and must find its own way, I do believe the following are essential steps on the path to establishing a needs based salary system on the basis of the threefold nature of community:

1) There must be a will within the teaching and the administrative staff, the board, and the relevant parent body to come to an understanding of the threefold nature of social life and on that understanding to build the life, form, and structure of the school. It will not succeed if this interests only a small group; the will to do so must live strongly within the school as a whole. This does not mean that everyone has to be fully involved, but all must stand behind those that do take up the impulse. They must "will" them to do so on behalf of the whole, and each must "take responsibility" for what results. Those who do become active will have to carry the others with them.

2) It is not possible to develop any one of the three sectors of social life in isolation; all three must be developed along side each other. If a person is to accept not only that she will receive what she needs, but that her colleagues will also receive what they need with all that that involves, then what was discussed in Chapters Eleven, Twelve, and Thirteen will have to have been brought to a certain reality in the school. The experience of freedom and equality and of being seen and valued as a unique individual by her colleagues will become a sustaining and creative force within each member. She will no longer need to look to her salary as that which gives her purpose, identity, and security for the future.

3) Three assumptions discussed earlier and fundamental to what is put forward in this book must be recognized as true. Firstly, the salary of a teacher or other cultural worker is not a purchase. Secondly, it is of the nature of a gift or contribution, one that frees a person to do certain work that is not itself "economic" work. Thirdly, such a contribution can only be related to the needs of that person.

4) The thought that each colleague is an "owner," not an "employee" must live strongly in the whole school. Even if it is necessary that some other body legally own the school, it should still be possible to develop the feeling that the relationship to the school is one not of an employee, but of one who owns it in the sense that she is responsible for it.

5) Most of us talk quite easily about karma and destiny. But do we truly accept them in all their reality? It is interesting how often our recognition of spiritual truths falls apart when it comes up against the everyday world of money. Ahriman has a field day there. If one person is to accept the fact that another might have comparatively greater needs than she has, and, therefore, be paid more, for the majority of people this will only be acceptable on a firm basis of a recognition of karma. The working of karma has to be recognized as a fact, and that needs are connected to the karma of the individual, whose needs must, therefore, be seen as real. Although one person cannot see the karma of another, she can know its reality and, therefore, accept it.

It is good to recognize from the beginning that the change will take several years to complete and for this to be taken into account in the planning. The intention to change and the activity of moving towards the goal will itself create life forces within the school. The importance of this should not be underestimated. The fact that there is an actual search for the truth and an active will to bring spiritual reality into the whole of the school beyond the classroom will itself shine forth from the school. The imaginative picture of what it is intended to achieve must be kept alive there as a goal.

I remember when, many years ago, I was myself building a room onto my house. My son, then about ten years old, was helping me. One hot Saturday we had been working all morning mixing cement and laying bricks. It was tiring work. After a good lunch and a sit down, it was very difficult to get up again and continue the work. My son made a very interesting observation which has remained with me. He said one must not look at the work still to be done. That makes one feel tired. One must imagine the finished room. It was remarkable how that imagination of what was coming into being seemed itself to actually lift us out of our seats to get on with it.

In my view all these things need to be worked on by the community, not just once or occasionally, but consistently over an extended period. The imaginative picture of what it is that the school is intending to reach should be constantly re-enlivened. There are a number of people and organizations, far more able than myself, who could help a school in the actual details of how to do this. It is to a great extent a matter of group work and individual development.

The question of what is a "need" is one that must be clarified. This has already been discussed from the perspective of the rights sphere in Chapter Fourteen. The agreement to pay salaries based on need and the standard of living considered reasonable must be something that comes out of the rights sphere of the school; that is, it arises out of the general feeling life of the community.

What people feel is a reasonable standard of living for the members of staff to expect is one thing. The money for the salaries that can be found from fees or other sources is another. Between these there has to come about a meeting of "rights" and "economic." But this seldom really happens, and sometimes the gap can become a real problem. But as was mentioned before, it makes an enormous difference if a person approaches the problem out of the feeling that she sells her labor, and the proper price is not paid, or that she recognizes she is doing the work that she herself chose and wants to do, and that the salary makes this possible. It is generally only in the latter case that a person may find the strength to continue without feeling let down, or "used."

There is a wide variation of ways of paying on a basis of need. At one end is having a carefully worked out but fixed scale with increments based purely on various needs, such as the number of children, and if there are one or two parents working, etc. At the other is allowing each person to decide for themselves their salary, or to have a common "pot," and each takes out of it what she wants. There can be many variations between these two extremes.

Salaries According to a Scale

My own feeling is that although a salary scale based on needs is a step in the right direction, it still has many problems and does not go far enough.

It recognizes only the outer factors, such as marital status and number of dependents. It takes no account of the fact that people are in themselves different. People are individual with individual karma and so have individual needs. One person may well have a real need for some kind of security, such as insurance and an extra pension. The need for this can be very real and failure to acknowledge it may lead to feelings of insecurity and worry. Another may need to feel well dressed. This should not be brushed aside as a fad. It can be a very real need arising out of a person's inner soul life. It might be something that she has a karmic need to overcome. She will succeed only if she can do this for herself. It is a wonderful thing when we can provide for each other the possibility to face our karma in freedom. Another person may well have no such needs, or even may have a need to live a simple life.

There is frequently a tendency to include a person's qualifications and length of service, but these seldom relate to need but to the value of the work.

It would take a most complex computer program to take account of all the possible variations of need to make a salary scale even approximately equitable. I doubt even then it would succeed. At regular intervals it would have to be reassessed to take account of changing social and economic conditions.

It is a very different experience, if a person's needs are calculated by fitting her into a category on a scale in a book or by looking her in the eye and recognizing her unique situation.

On the positive side a scale, by the fact that it is impersonal, applies to every one equally and can be seen and understood by all, is sometimes experienced as more transparent and equitable. There is a lot of truth in this. But it is achieved by dehumanizing the process, by denying the individual karma, the soul capacities, and needs of each person. Is that what is wanted? Surely our intention should be to make it more human, in that it is experienced as recognizing the free and individual human being.

In a certain sense the conventional "purchase of labor" salaries do at least recognize the different individual qualities and capacities of each person, whereas a needs based scale fails to do this. It sees every individual's inner soul nature as the same, only their outer economic status as differing. To establish a scale taking account of different needs arising out of the individual karma and soul nature of each human being is an impossibility.

It might be helpful at this point to bring something of an experience we had about five years ago at Emerson. I had become aware that there were some colleagues who had questions concerning the basis of our salaries. Some felt that a scale would be more transparent and equitable. I began to wonder whether there really was a will to continue on the existing basis of not having any scale but working on individual assessment. It was in any case time for a review of the whole sphere of salaries, especially as I would be retiring the following year.

We formed a group of five to do this. We decided to look at what it would mean to create a needs based scale and pay everyone on that. We spent some time working on this scale, taking into account all the factors that we could, not only the obvious ones such as children, but also, for example, where the college provided housing, with the advantages and disadvantages that gave. We eventually arrived at the best we could achieve, although not really as good as we would have liked considering all the possible variations.

We then started to put our colleagues into this scale. I always remember the reaction from the others in the group. I had kept my own thoughts to myself. Putting people into the scale meant that, although overall it would cost the college more, some people would in future get less and others more than they did at that time. As we looked at each person's actual life situation and what this would mean for them, the feeling was strongly expressed that "we cannot do this to people," that "it is inhuman to categorize people like this." Such comments came particularly strongly from those who had had questions about our present system.

It was then decided to recommend that we continue with the existing way of arriving at salaries by individual assessment, but with some, though less radical, changes. This was accepted by the staff as a whole almost without question.

No Salary Scale - Individual Assessment

The other possibility is one of salaries based on individual assessment, either by the individual himself, by a committee of colleagues, or between the two. This is the most difficult. It means that the actual life situation of each individual and of the institution has to be faced quite directly. But in my experience, it leads to by far the most individually fulfilling and productive working community.

The first difficulty is to come to a sense of what is a reasonable "need" in the particular community. If in discussions you were asked in connection with your application to work in a school, "What do you need?" – what would be your answer? This is always a difficult question. A person wants to adjust to the community into which she would be entering. I was often asked the question, "What is the average salary for someone in my life situation?" Many needs are relative to the community in which a person lives and works. Because a person needs good clothes in a community where everyone dresses well and always looks smart does not mean that she will need the same clothes when she moves to a community where few even have smart clothes.

Many other questions will arise that will need to be resolved. One such will be does the "need" include an amount for unforeseen necessary expenditures, such as a sudden large re-pair bill for the car or house? Or can it be a flexible arrangement where a person asks for what she knows she will need, knowing that if and when reasonable unforeseen expenditure is needed, she will be given it. If this is what is agreed, it should be seen not as the school helping the colleague, nor as giving out charity, but as no more than the school meeting needs as agreed.

In each member of staff the thought must be kept alive: "This is my work, and I wish to continue to be active in it here at this school. What do I need that I may continue this work? If necessary, can I and my colleagues adjust our needs so that they are within what the school (or parents) can provide, in order that the school and our work can continue? If the school cannot continue and closes, I will not be able to continue this work I have chosen."

If these thoughts are kept alive and real, then it will be possible, when problems arise, to find reasonable solutions.

A person coming new into a community will need to be given help and time to develop a "sense" of the generally ac-cepted standard of living within that community and also of the financial situation and possibilities of the school. It may be nec-essary, after discussion, to suggest a figure to him, but a time for review should always be agreed. It should also be recognized that there is always the possibility that the school will not be in a position to meet needs asked for.

Full or Part Time

A salary that is based on a person's needs rather than on the actual work done cannot, therefore, be determined by the length of time worked. But the school cannot be expected to meet the full needs of people who only work part time. How then is it decided when a person is "full time"? What about those who work part time, and how does one determine when a person is one or the other?

Full time can only be a full commitment to the work of the school, or a commitment to put all their work, or their main work, into the school. The actual hours will vary from person to person, and, according to the nature of the work, it will not be possible to actually establish a "number of hours," if the individual is to work in freedom out of their own impulses and capacities.

Of course, it is also good that people make connections with and work in other institutions. Then it must be decided: does the school provide their whole needs and what they earn elsewhere then goes to the school, or do they ask the school for their needs less what they can provide from other sources? For part time people one can

1) try to determine the proportion their work is to a full time commitment and cover the same proportion of their needs. This is more suitable for people who work a substantial time at the school on an ongoing basis.

2) or pay the person by the hour. Here one can still establish an individual hourly rate based on the needs of the person, but calculate it hourly as a matter of administrative convenience. Or one can pay a general "rate for the job" or some other general rate. Here it should be understood by both parties that the intention would be to meet the needs, but in the circumstances this is the only practical way of doing this. For some people from outside the school circles this might be the only acceptable way.

One Way to Start

Emerson College has worked this way from the beginning, so we have not been through any process of changing over to needs based salaries. But from the experience I have had and from discussions with others, I have come to the opinion that the process is more likely to succeed if it is gradual. It will presumably start from some sort of fixed salaries based on a scale. Without precipitously scraping this, flexibility can be brought in by recognizing those people who suffer most under the system and over a period gradually adjusting their salaries to take into account their personal situations. Scaled annual increases can be reduced and slowly faded out as everyone comes into individual consideration.

To do this each member of staff could be asked to individually meet with the salary committee. But as far as possible this should be experienced, not as a meeting with a "committee," but as a meeting with a group of her colleagues, who are interested in her situation, including how her work is going, and, for instance, whether her expectations when she came to the school have been fulfilled. When a person feels that she is in truth talking to colleagues who are really interested in her welfare and who value her as a colleague, she is far more likely to think twice as to whether she really does need what she first thought she did. She will be able to look at her needs in a much more objective way and not be shy of saying what she really does need. If she experiences that the intention is to give her what she asks for, in so far as this is reasonable and possible, then when asked what she needs, she will ask for the minimum. In my experience if one is open and honest with people, then they will be open and honest with oneself.

In actual practice our experience here has been that people adjust to this way of salaries far more readily than might be expected. There is something in the human being that in the unconscious depths of the soul recognizes it as true and as that which leaves one free. It is only when concepts and theories derived from modern social and economic thinking take hold that people have problems. I have often explained how we calculate salaries to visitors to the College, whether building workmen, tax inspectors, or salespeople. I have been surprised how often they have wished they could work that way. I have sensed a kind of envy.

Whatever salary system one uses, there will be problems. We certainly have them at Emerson. But from my observations we do not have them to the extent that I see in many schools. But there they are often hidden by the fact of the fixed scale that has a certain inevitability about it against which it is difficult to complain about individual hardships, except in general terms.

Just as the successful work of the school will depend on achieving freedom in the cultural sphere and equality in the rights, it will not be possible to come to these two principles with any effect, unless there is also mutuality or brotherhood in the economic sphere. That means, in a cultural institution, the necessity to get away from purchasing a person's work, but to pay according to individual and personal needs.

The question as to whether each person should know what others receive was discussed in Chapter Fourteen. In my opinion it is only possible and beneficial in a very small community to work on such a basis, and then there must be a close and confident relationship between all. Otherwise, I would strongly advise against it. It is far better that a small group in whom everyone has confidence should be formed to look after salaries. Their work would be not only to question those who seem to need an amount that places an undue burden on the whole, but also to see that people are looking after themselves and do ask for enough for their needs. Otherwise, they may be building up problems for the future.

But it is important that the overall finances of the school are brought to the staff on a regular basis in a form that is easily understood by everyone. The consciousness of the money as it comes and goes should be something that all feel connected to and responsible for. After all, whatever they ask for as salary has an effect on the accounts. It has to come from somewhere.

Needs Based and the Law of Discrimination

In some countries, such as the U.S.A., certain types of needs based salary arrangements would be illegal, so it may be advisable to seek legal advise. A scale which clearly gives a person with a spouse more pay than the one without would be seen, in law, as discriminating against the single person who would be seen to be paid less for the same work. This probably means that there can be no scale for salaries based on needs.

I understand that where there is no scale, but where every employment is individually contracted and where it is the employee who states that she will work for a particular salary, one not derived from any scale based on needs, then it would not fall foul of the law. The fact that the employee may base her request on what she needs is her concern and cannot, therefore, be seen as discriminatory.

Chapter Eighteen

Fees and the Working of Destiny

Fees and salaries are to a large extent two sides of the same transaction. Much of what has been said about salaries is also true of fees. But whereas it is possible to work towards paying salaries on a needs basis, much as we might like to do so, it is at present seldom possible to consider charging fees purely on the basis of what each family can afford. In the parent body of almost every Waldorf school there is a very widespread range of interest in Anthroposophy or in working out of a new social impulse. But despite this, within the school and amongst some of the parents, there will be those who can or do recognize certain truths, and some steps can be taken towards bringing a healthier approach and way of working into the sphere of fees or parent contribution.

First, I would like to look at something that some might consider as going too far from the practical realities of life. But in my view it is essentially practical, and that to ignore it is itself impractical. Karma, destiny, and the hierarchies of Spiritual Beings are just as real and work into our daily lives as do money, our physical environment, and automobiles.

The Fee as Gift Capital

We saw in Chapter Three that a fee is really a contribution towards the cost of running the school. In Chapter Seven we saw that what the school as an institution within cultural life receives is really what we should call "gift capital." In the case of the fee perhaps we should say "of the nature of gift capital." This is money that can make possible the working of destiny. The question is how to work with money in a way that provides the freedom for this to happen.

What does this mean? Can we really recognize this and know it, or at least just believe it, to be true?

As bursar at Emerson, I often had to deal with personal questions concerning money. All too often I had the experience of a person leaving her "Anthroposophy" outside on the other side of the threshold of my office when she brought her money or legal questions in to me. This even included people whose commitment to Anthroposophy and the work of the College or the school I recognized and deeply respected. They divided their lives between two worlds: the world where the spirit, which was the basis of their life and work, was fully acknowledged and in a very real way taken into consideration, and the world of everyday affairs, of those matters which concern money, economic, and legal matters.

But these are not two worlds; they are one. If we fail to recognize this and deny the reality of the spirit when we work with money, then we open the doors to those Spirit Beings who strive to hinder our work, to bring egoism, untruths, and division into our institutions.

The Working of Karma?

Karma works in manifold ways. There might well be times when one human soul, to fulfill a karmic responsibility, wills to connect herself to another human soul, perhaps by giving support to the school which has accepted that soul as a child. These things work through our will, through the unconscious depths of our actions. The giving of money is one form of the expression of such karmic will impulses.

There were many times when a young man or woman would apply to the College for admittance but did not have enough money. The question then was whether it was truly willed out of the spiritual world and the working of human destiny that this person attend the College.

The spiritual world will not indicate to us that if we accept this young person who cannot pay, on this occasion money will be given from another source, or there will be enough income for the College anyway. That might have been what would have happened in past ages, but not now in our time. Now we have earnestly to try to perceive what it is that brings her to this College. Is this a destiny situation? Only after we have made the decision might support come, and destiny be fulfilled. Or it may not come.

We live in the Michaelic age. On one level this means that the spiritual world no longer leads human beings. It waits for us first to act; only then will it support or hold back. Before making a decision we cannot first look for guidance to the higher hierarchies. We must take full responsibility for our own actions, and we must make the decision. Only then can spiritual beings respond.

Francis Edmunds often spoke of Emerson College being willed out of the spiritual world. It was not "his" college. It was his task to bring into being a place that was needed at this time, a place to which young people could come in order to prepare themselves to fulfill those resolutions they made during pre-birth existence, resolutions for work that they would come to in later years. He sometimes said that Emerson College was a place where young people would come "to remember their task."

And so when someone came asking for admission, who had little or no money, the question would arise, "Is this someone for whom the College was founded?" This was always a difficult decision to make, to recognize if this particular young person "should" be at the College. There were also those who came for other reasons - because it was a "nice place," or a haven from the harshness of the world. The College was not founded for them.

It would not necessarily be that someone would give money specifically for such a person who we decided to accept into the College. After all, one more in the class did not increase the cost to any effect. If we were heading for a deficit, that would be there whether or not we accepted the student. But it could well be that other students would come due to the fact that we had accepted the one, or that a donation was made to the College that would not have been made if that particular student had not been accepted.

Of course, we can always think that such things would have happened anyway. How are we to know that karma is at work? But in my observation there has been too often a pattern behind events for it to be mere coincidence. There appears a beauty and an artistic wholeness about life's events that is not haphazard. Let me give, very briefly, two examples out of many that I observed, two small components of a greater tableau. In themselves they could be coincidences, but in the wider panorama of experience they make a picture that shows something quite different.

First, during the summer term I would interview those students who did not have enough money for the fees for the following year, but who wished to return for further training, and where the teachers involved felt they should return, that their future work was in some way important. I would first try to establish how much money they had and thought they could find. I would often have to bring pressure on them to think of new ways to find money. Then, depending on the particular individual and the circumstances, I would give them a figure that would stretch them but which I felt was within the possibilities of their finding. They then knew that if they found that extra money, they would be accepted on the agreed reduced contribution.

On this occasion two young women needed reductions. One from the U.S.A. had only a very little money, and for various reasons was not in a position to earn much, and her parents could not help. I found that she did have a godmother who had money, but, "I don't like to ask, I am not close with her, and she will not approve of what I am doing." I told her that if she was prepared to ask the College, she should be prepared to ask her godmother. I felt that she must make an effort to find more and gave her a fairly high figure she really would have to find if she intended to return.

The second young woman was from Canada. She had a little money of her own. Her father was going to give her some, and she would have a job so would earn more. She would be living at home, so could save her earnings. She thought she would have most of the fees but might not quite manage all. We agreed a minimum figure, if she could not find it all.

Half way through the summer the Canadian woman phoned to say her father had become very ill and had also lost his job. He, therefore, could not give what he had offered. She could not work, as she had to stay at home to look after him. She would have almost no money so would not return. After discussions we told her that she should return and to bring whatever money she could manage.

I always remember on the first day of the new year, when the young woman from U.S.A. came up to me with a big smile in her eyes to say that she had plucked up courage and had asked her godmother, who agreed to pay the full fee. So the amount the College received in fees was as originally agreed, but it came from a different source.

On this occasion the balance was achieved clearly between the two. But every year such a balance was achieved over all those students intending to return. The individual circumstances and amounts changed, but the overall total remained basically the same. For me there was often the question, for example, if we had not accepted the Canadian woman on almost no money, would the godmother have agreed to pay the whole fee? We can never know. But this sort of thing happened too often to be explained by coincidence.

The second example was what followed when we accepted a young woman from abroad who had no money. We did find ways to cover her board and lodging costs, but for two years we received no tuition fees at all. The whole circumstance of her finding her way to the College, the quiet quality which pervaded her and gave promise for the future, all contributed to the picture that she was a person "for whom the College was created."

In the years following many young people came to us as a direct consequence of this young woman's activities to carry Anthroposophy and Waldorf education to her country. These others could and did pay the normal fee. There was no way we could know, when she first applied, what was intended for the future and that a whole new area of work would develop out of her coming to the College.

It was as though she had to find the way for those to whom she was connected through her karma and who would follow after her. But she had to be allowed entry. Those who followed would bring what the College needed. It could not be the money that decided whether she should be accepted, but an intuitive recognition of her destiny. There are times when to bring strength to the unfolding of certain human destiny work, it is necessary that others have to connect their own will to it out of their own intuitions. In such times this can only happen when there is an obstacle to overcome, such as there being no money. The money would follow the decision, not precede it.

Karma also in the School

Many might think that this may be true for an institution of adult education, but how does it relate to a school which is of quite a different nature? One might think that in a school such connections just would not happen.

But karma is also there behind the interconnections in a school. What brings a family to decide to send their child to a particular school? What are the connections that parents and former students make to the wider public? What prompts a person to give money, or to talk of the school to a friend or at a casual meeting? Observation will confirm that though it manifests in other ways, the spiritual world is also there acting according to what is made possible through the decisions and work in a school, differently, but there, too. What is important is that the school sets out to observe what happens when they free up the fee structure, when they really do work with fees according to their true nature.

There is a further point concerning the question of whether to consider accepting children who cannot contribute the full fees to a class, when there are others that can pay, but who would be thereby excluded.

Most people who have carried a course in adult education have found that it soon takes on a certain character. It develops a particular structure, a balance in the interplay of temperaments, attributes, and the needs and gifts of the participants. One begins to see that there is a certain cohesion, a wholeness about the group of people that make up the course, and one senses that there is a wisdom behind its formation. I am sure this is also true for a class of children, as it is for adult students. The experience of the particular group, what they learn by being in it with these particular children, can also be an essential and necessary part of their education.

To illustrate something of this nature of a group, I would like to give two illustrations.

Some years ago I heard a lecture on the work of the Camphill Homes given by the late Doctor Thomas Weiss. He explained how the children with different handicaps helped and supported each other. They had found that there was a particular ratio or balance between the various handicaps that worked most effectively for the social life of the group as a whole. One of the audience asked the question that if children were accepted into such homes on the basis of such a ratio, then there would be some children left out. I was very struck when Dr. Weiss pointed out that this was not so, as they had found that the healthy ratio for the group was the same as the ratio such handicaps were to be found in the wider community. It struck me forcibly then that there was a wisdom behind these things, that life was not haphazard.

A Second Characterization.

In one particular course with which I was involved, this was particularly pronounced. Although the participants were all very different, I sensed that they all had a connection, that it was a group karmically connected. There was one particular student whose reason for coming to this particular course I could not quite understand. She appeared to have almost no connection to the actual theme. But she was part of the group, and without her something would have been missing. Part of the experience of being in the group would have been lost. I came to the conclusion that she had come to be with the others, not for the subject matter of the course.

This does not mean that every such group or class is a karmic group, or that each person within such a group has a karmic connection to all the others. But there is a wisdom behind the forming of such groups; I cannot believe that their coming together is always accidental or haphazard.

Nor can I believe that by accepting only those who can pay full fees we are providing the space needed for this wisdom to work. The class will not then be formed as it might have been, and there will not be the wholeness that was intended.

What of the child born into a poor family who also needs, out of her own and a particular teacher's karma, to work with that teacher?

All this will, of course, leave many questions. Only a careful study and observation of life can lead to answers and confirmation or otherwise of what has been said here.

Chapter Nineteen

Fees - A Share of the Cost

Economically, the school, which includes all those who work there - the teaching and administrative staff - is a consumer of economic products. It produces very little itself. It is a producer of economic products only to the extent that it is itself active in such things as preparing meals or in cleaning, heating, and repairing its own buildings and environment. It is the activity of those working in economic life in the wider world that provides the school and staff with the products they need. These needs consist mainly of what the staff must have to live: housing, clothes, food, cars, books, and travel, etc. The school also needs teaching aids and materials, heat, power, and such things as office supplies. These are all provided by the economic life of the world to the extent that the parents, and possibly others, contribute money as fees, gifts, or grants to the school. Some of this is passed on to the individual members of staff as salaries.

It is important that we see clearly what it is that actually happens. The paying and receiving of money is not itself an economic activity. The money is that which gives the school or individual a right to, or power to acquire, the products of other people's labor. It connects them to the wider world without which the school could not exist. Without this money the individuals would have to find other work in order to support themselves. They would not be free to teach.

Economically, the money frees the teacher to teach by giving her a right to products that others have produced. It is not the purpose of the school to earn money; that is necessary but not its purpose. It is no more necessary than that it is needed to enable the school to fulfill its purpose of teaching children.

Shared Cost

We saw earlier, particularly in Chapter Three, that the fee which the parent pays to the school is not the price of a purchase. There is no exchange of economic products. The teacher does what she does, because that is her work, in so far as she is rightfully there. The fee that the parent gives to the school is, in fact, a gift or contribution to help pay the costs the teacher has, so that she is free to teach the children.

Most of us are on familiar ground with the idea of purchase and sale. But with contribution or gift we are dealing with something quite different, and here many feel themselves on uncertain ground.

We can look at this from another perspective.

When I was bursar, I gave a talk each year to the students on the College finances, including an outline of the accounts. This included a description of the way we worked with the fees. Although more relevant for a college of adult education, it will be illustrative to give something of that picture here.

Imagine that it costs $10,000 to run a college for 100 students, excluding all individual costs, such as student meals and room. That means the fee should be $100.

But let us assume that although there are a number of students who want to attend, there are not 100 but only 80 who can pay $100. As it will cost basically the same to run the college whether there are 80 or 100 students, the 80 would then have to pay $125 each.

Now suppose that there are in addition to the 80 who can pay the full fee, 10 potential students who could pay $75 each and another 10 able to pay $50. If these were accepted at a reduced fee of what they could afford, many people would say that the 80 paying full fees would be subsidizing the 20 who pay less. But is that true? By accepting those who would pay less, the fees of the others would actually be reduced. The 80 would then have to pay not $125 but just under $110. We could even say that those who pay less subsidize those who pay more.

Both statements are equally inadequate to explain the reality. We cannot say that either subsidizes the other. That would only be true if there were an actual cost per person. As soon as we think in terms of a "cost" per person, we will find ourselves in all sorts of contradictions, because there is not a cost per person.

At most we could say that there would be a cost for the first student. For that one there is the total cost of running the course. When the next student joins the course there is basically no extra "cost," apart from a few art materials, etc. The cost is for the course or class, not for each student. After the first we can then only talk in terms of "sharing the cost."

But cost should not be confused with purchase. There is a cost of running a course but there is no exchange, no purchase. The needs of the teacher must be met, and heat and light provided. A "fee" is in reality a share of the total cost, that which has to be given or contributed.

In the school there is the fact that class sizes are limited, so the situation can arise where there are, or would be, enough children to fill the class whose parents could afford to contribute the full fee asked. But it is still true that the fee is a share of the cost, not an actual cost. Each student or family agrees to contribute a share of the total costs. The question then arises as to whether each family should contribute an "equal" or the "same" share, and whether only those children whose parents could afford such a share should be admitted to the class.

Is "Same" Fair or Equitable?

Today there is much talk and striving for "equality." But is "equal" the same as "fair"?

What do we mean by "fair" or "equitable"? Is life and the society in which we live "fair"? One person may work hard, and her work be of considerable benefit to the community. Her karma may have led her to such work in a sphere of social life where she will be paid, say, only $30,000 per year. Another, without working any harder and whose work may not be of such benefit to the community, might earn $50,000. A third, without doing any "work" at all - one who lives on inherited investments – has an income of $60,000. Is "fairness" that they each pay the same "mathematical" amount - say $10,000, or that they each pay the same "proportion" of their income? Why is the first always thought to be fair, and the second unfair? Why not the other way round? Could not the second be said to be more fair than the first?

Of course, we are used to thinking in terms of mathematics, that only same amounts are equal. But reality is not as simple as that. We have to see that in life often different amounts are equal and fair, and the same amounts are unequal or unfair. "Equality" does not demand or mean "sameness." To think so will again lead one into all sorts of strange contradictions.

Life and our present society do not make it possible for all people to have the same income, and if we are to be true to life, why do they have to contribute the same amount? We must find a way for students or parents to pay an amount that is true to life. This is particularly pertinent at a place like Emerson, where we have students from rich industrially developed countries as well as from poor African, East European, and Asian countries. But the same divide is to be found in many of the cities and communities of even the most economically developed and rich countries.

A fee is a share of the cost, or we can say that it is a contribution towards the total cost. We can call it a "contracted contribution." The parent contracts to contribute an agreed amount, and the school contracts to run the necessary classes and to accept the child into them. That is the term nearest to the reality that I have found. We cannot call it simply a gift or free gift. If it is not paid, the school will rightly demand that what is owed be paid, and if necessary, may even have to taken legal action to obtain payment. If it is called a gift, then payment cannot be demanded. We need to find words that are as true as possible to what we think and mean, to our concepts.

If we accept that what has been said so far is true, then can we use such terms as "scholarship" or "scholarship fund," or fee "assistance"? Whatever we may think or know, if we use these terms, we are implying that there is a "cost" that the parent cannot pay, and, therefore, they need help in meeting that cost. The thought of education being a product that can be bought and sold is then sustained in the school, though in a hidden way.

It is, of course, much easier to establish a fixed fee, treat it as an actual cost, and insist that each parent pay that amount, perhaps on a sliding scale for any following siblings. Then a fund can be set up to help those who cannot meet the cost of the fee. When the fund is empty, no more help can be given. It also makes it easier to raise funds "to help individual children from poor backgrounds to go to a Waldorf school." People do prefer to give to specific causes, more so if they can know which actual children they are helping. This conforms with the way the great majority of people think. It comes out of the culture of our time, of thinking in terms of economic life. People think this way, and for them it is the reality, and that they do think so is also a reality.

But we have seen that in actual fact it is not so, that such a way of dealing with fees is not true to objective reality, that it has its consequences in fostering economic thinking as a basic thought structure in the school and in society.

The foundation of the Waldorf school, the basis out of which it finds its purpose, is the recognition of the supersensible, Spiritual Beings behind all earthly existence. The school, too, has its Spiritual Being, and untruths in the work of the school have their effect.

How Can the Cost be Shared?

If it is accepted that the fee is not the price of a purchase, but is in reality a share of a total cost, then on what basis can the share that each should pay be calculated? This question is one of rights; that is, is it fair and equitable that each should contribute the same amount, or should each contribute an amount relative to what he can afford?

The answer to this must come out of, or at least be recognized and supported by, the parents themselves. Here it will be important that some sort of dialogue is brought about within the parent body and with the staff of the school to grapple with this question. Out of Anthroposophy we might come to the conclusion that a fee structure based on the ability to pay is the one most true to both what is equitable and to economics as outlined here. But we cannot just impose this on the parents.

We cannot ignore the way people think and dogmatically insist that they change. Rather, we have to find a way of working with two factors, that is, the reality of what is, and the reality of the way people think. We have to find our way from the one to the other. We can only change our forms and systems in the school as we, that is, the staff and the parents of the school, learn to know what is true and real and what is not. People can only work fruitfully in one way or another, when they know or believe that way to be true. People do have a feeling for the actual truth, and if we can use the right terminology, form our structures within the school, and regulate our actions according to what we see as true reality, then others will come to see it for themselves. They do not have to be anthroposophists, or even believe in a spiritual world to come to see that education is not an economic product that can be bought and sold, or that sameness is not necessarily fair.

If it is decided to move to a fee structure based on ability to contribute, then the next question will be whether this should be on a predetermined sliding scale according to income, left entirely to the individual parent, or somewhere in between these two.

As I said earlier, I cannot speak from my own experience here, but from observation and discussions in schools I would strongly recommend going extremely slowly towards freeing up the fees, or what can more properly be called the parental contributions to the school. Any move would need to be in conjunction with the parents and be what they feel comfortable with.

Schools vary very widely with regards to the nature of the problem and of the parent body. This can range from the school that is full and exists in a wealthy area where parents do not have a problem with the fees, to one in a poor area where classes are never full, or to where there is a community of anthroposophical activities or a new age community, from a large urban area where few parents know each other, to a small rural area where every one knows each other. There are many more extremes. It is impossible to give more than very general ideas. Every school will have to find its own way of working within the possibilities presented by its particular situation.

But some thoughts:

1) One possibility is to actually pitch the fee higher than would be needed if all paid it. This would mean that those who could afford to pay more did so by paying the normal fee. There would then be scope to reduce it for those who could afford less.

2) I would tend to avoid setting a low fee hoping some will pay more. Not many do, but those that do often see it as being charitable to those who are poorer. This can create varying degrees of emotional conflicts in the parent body.

3) There should always be a minimum contribution. Rules should never be absolute, but this minimum should only be breached in exceptional cases.

4) A scheme where parents can contribute by working to cover part of their fees can be a very fruitful idea, but the work must be something that is needed and which, if not done, would incur expenditure by the school. Otherwise, it may be very nice to have the particular work done, but it would not help the school financially, so could not be thought of as an alternative to paying the fee.

Perhaps the two most important things that should be taken fully into the consciousness of all concerned, teachers and administrative staff, as well as where possible the parents, are: First, the purpose of the school is to teach children, as many as want to come and that it is possible to teach. It is not the purpose of the school to make money. It needs money in order to fulfill its task, for no other reason.

And second, the fee the parents pay is a contracted contribution, not a purchase. It is not the price of education. If these two facts are recognized as true, the rest will follow, and people will soon come to know how to act.

Chapter Twenty

The Accounts and Administration

It is not my intention to go into detail as to the keeping of accounts and the control of the finances. But some comments may be helpful.

In working with money there are two dangers for which we must be constantly alert. These are the strong temptations of going too far, on the one side, in the way set out by Ahriman and, on the other, in that direction influenced by Lucifer. Schools do not often go in as extreme a way as I shall illustrate here, but it will help to show what can happen.

The Ahrimanic Way

On the one side there is the tendency to separate the teaching and business functions in a school. What happens is that those activities and decisions relating to the teaching are carried by the teachers and are based on all that spiritual science has to tell us. But the financial business is left to those who understand it according to the standards of modern economic science and good business management. Decisions are made according to the numbers in the accounts, which act as the final arbiter in all matters where finances are involved. It is assumed that Spiritual Science has nothing to contribute in this field.

A budget is drawn up at the beginning of each year, which determines what is to be spent in each department. This is a budget in the sense that all expenditure is predetermined by the finance committee.

In such a budget there is no place for the working of karma and destiny or of those resolves that individuals bring with them through birth from worlds of spirit. If money was not allocated for a particular event, or if there is not other money found, then it cannot happen during the current budget period. It will have to be budgeted for the following year. Only those children can be admitted for whom full fees are paid, or where there are sufficient scholarships or other funds to make up the full fee. To accept children without full fees is a cost to the school and places a financial burden on other parents, which is unfair and inequitable.

There is often a fear of the unknown, of taking a step into the dark without clear knowledge of what lies ahead – a fear of not being in full control, of being held responsible for mistakes which will come about when freedom is given for the unknown to work. On the other hand, there is a feeling of security in the logic of, and discipline established by, the accounts.

There will also grow the tendency to assume that anyone who cannot pay the full fee is "getting away" with something, that one has been weak to allow it.

The Luciferic Way

Then there is the second danger, the Luciferic way of working. This is to pay too little attention to the actual accounts and to make all decisions based more on the cultural aims of the school and with what the teachers feel is right, rather than on the figures in the books. Sometimes there develops a belief, often unconscious but nevertheless there, that if the school works according to the spiritual world, that if it works anthroposophically, all will be well, and the gods will provide.

How often do we want to follow just our feelings? There can be an impulse to accept without further question a new family who arrives, full of warmth and spirituality, and who wants to put their children in the school and who are "sure they will find the fees." There is also a tendency to believe that money is Ahrimanic, that one should not be led by it, or allow it to influence decisions on spiritual questions.

This way is often fostered by a fear of knowing, a fear of the discipline imposed by the mathematics of accounts. The unknown allows for a belief that the spiritual world will provide, and that it will all work out right.

The Balance between the Two

Neither of these two ways are always wrong. They are only so when followed one sidedly. We need something of both, but in balance. We must have correct and exact accounts that inform us of the financial state of the school. We must know the apparent financial consequences of any decision we take, and we must take responsibility for those consequences. That something feels right, or is a lovely idea, is not enough by itself.

But we must also know that the accounts tell us what has happened in the past, not what "wills" to come out of the future. We need to find ways to know what this is that comes towards us and to make space for it to happen.

The thought can arise that people who cannot pay the full "price" are a failure in life, and it is charitable to help them. It gives people a feeling of being good when they are able to think that they are being charitable.

But is there another "truth"?

I remember one occasion when this was brought home to me. We had at the College a married student couple. They had worked out their finances and could pay for their year. Half way through the year they came to me to say they would have to leave. Apparently due to events outside their control, their financial arrangements had fallen through, and they no longer had sufficient money for the remainder of the year. They had already paid the fees due till then. They could find enough to cover their actual expenses of board and lodging but not for the tuition fees.

In considering the situation a number of things became apparent. First came the thought as to whether we should be charitable and help them. They were, after all "one of us," and surely it was always right to help people. The spiritual world must look favorably on such an act of faith.

But then it came as an interesting realization that we would not actually save any money by their leaving, nor would there be an actual cost if they stayed. Financially, it made little difference whether they stayed or left. But we would lose in another way; that is, we would not be able to do that work which we had set ourselves as our central purpose. This purpose was to work with those students who came looking for their spiritual path and to prepare themselves for their future work, work that would also be for humanity. Here were two people who clearly filled this need. But if they left, we could not work with them.

Then came the suspicion that they might be trying it on; if they really tried, they could find the money, that they knew the way we worked and so hoped we would help them. There was also the suspicion that if we allowed them to stay, others would "try it on."

These two factors played strongly on our feelings. On the one side was that it would be "charitable to help them." This gave one a feeling of being good. On the other side was all that arises through feelings of suspicion and distrust. To act on these gave the feeling of being responsible, professional.

These two each pulled in different directions, but both tried to hide from us the true reality and to prevent us from doing our work. They hid the human beings and all that lived and worked in and through them.

We must always remember that there is a spiritual world, that karma and destiny are realities just as money is, and that we must have the courage to allow them to work, to make room for the unknown. That may take courage. But it must be a courage that is based on knowledge of the spirit, not on any emotions or simple belief. We must develop a sense for what wills to come about.

The Accounts

The school must keep accurate and detailed accounts of all moneys received and spent. But we must not confuse the accounts of an institution of the cultural life with those of a business or manufacturer or other organizations of economic life. As we saw in Chapter Five, an economic enterprise must aim to make a profit, and the need to do so is part of its very purpose. Failure to make a profit indicates that something is not working properly.

But the purpose of a school is to teach children. Making a profit does not lie within its purpose. The money enables it to fulfill its purpose. If it could do this without money, it would do so.

In a school the accounts have to be read and understood in a different way from those of an economic enterprise. Much is, of course, the same, but there are subtle differences which are important. For example, in a manufacturing enterprise the cost of each stage or activity must be established. This must be done in such a way that it shows the true price of that activity. Every such activity must show a profit. If it does not, then either the accounting is incorrect in that profit arising at a later stage, but due to this one, is not included, or it is failing to produce the production results intended. Then action has to be taken to remedy the situation and bring the activity into profit. Here the making of profit is the ultimate measure and aim.

In a school the making of profit, or a better word is "surplus," at any stage can only be an indicator that the school has the economic support it needs for its work. If the school is producing a deficit, this itself does not necessarily mean that the teaching is poor (it may be very good), nor does it mean that the aim or activity of the school must be changed. In such a situation it may be necessary to look for other ways to find the economic support needed for its work, which is seen as its sole purpose. But it could also indicate that the school is not alive to the needs of the children and the parents.

There is something else to the accounts of an institution of cultural life. They are a record of what has happened. They can reveal to anyone who can read them far more than just the amounts of money received and spent. A great deal can be seen through them of the life and activities of the school.

Reading the Accounts

I once saw a beautifully made film called "Between the Tides" of the stories behind the markings in the sand on the seashore. Through these marks one could see, for instance, where a crab had moved, how it had wondered across the sand, and where it had caught something. There had been a struggle. Then it had moved on, and one could see where suddenly a large bird had landed. Though the crab had tried to dash to the sea, it had in its turn been caught by the bird and carried away. All this activity of life and death, though itself unseen, was recorded and revealed in the markings in the sand to anyone who knew how to read them.

The accounts of a school have something of this nature; they are marks on the sand indicating the struggles and activity that has gone on, the life of the school and of those within and connected to it. One has to learn to read them.

When I joined it, the College was still young and small. The numbers of students and staff were much less than they grew to in later years. So also the accounts were comparatively simple. At first I did everything from opening the post, checking the invoices, making out and posting the checks, working out student fees, salaries, etc., to making all entries in the account books.

In doing all the entries myself I had my fingers on the pulse of the College. I was able to develop a sense of the movement of money through the College and through this to have a sense of what was happening and of the causes of growth or decline. I did not set a budget and keep monthly balances to see how we were doing. Two or three times a year I would do what I called a "projected balance of accounts." I would go through every ledger account and, based on what had happened so far in the College and what I knew of the likely events and happenings to come, I would project the income and expenditure for the rest of the year. To do this I needed also to know something of what new impulses lived in the teachers. Then from these totals I would calculate the projected surplus or deficit.

Occasionally, this came out quite differently from what I had "sensed" was the situation. On each occasion when this happened, on checking my figures I found that the main cause was a mistake in the calculations. My sense of the situation had always been reasonably accurate.

But as the College grew, and we took on an assistant who did much of the actual bookkeeping, it became more difficult to retain that sense for what was happening. When we computerized the accounts, it became more difficult still. It was only because I had developed the sensitivity over the years that I was able to a large extent to continue in this way. Of course, the development of the College, growing in size and complexity, did not help. I had to take steps to retain a sense of what was happening.

There is sometimes the tendency to "put the accounts out to an accountant," who will do all the actual work and then present the school with the completed accounts, probably on a monthly basis. I do believe that this is actually an inefficient way of working. It takes an extremely skilled person to "read" a finished set of accounts. Behind every total there is a story which has to be read. Only a person with some familiarity with the day to day working of the school and with the accounts can read them. Let me give a few examples out of my experience at Emerson. I am aware that Emerson is a more complex organization than most schools.

In the early days we could not afford to buy such things as curtains for all the windows of the teaching areas. One day a course leader asked if he could buy material for curtains for his classroom. They had found some material being sold cheap, and a student would make them free, so they it would only cost the College $20. That seemed too cheap to be able to say "no."

But I said that it was more likely to cost the College $200 rather than $20. As soon as one classroom had curtains, all the other windows would look bare beside it. There would then be a greatly increased pressure to put up curtains on all the other classroom windows, and it is doubtful if they could be done as cheaply as the one set.

One has to become very aware of these financial "pressures" that lead to expenditure in the future.

Again, I remember when we were considering inviting someone to teach at the College, who had a private income and would not want any salary. We had not been looking for such a teacher, but when she came forward and wanted to teach without a salary, it was of course very easy to be interested. This was not the first time we had been helped in this way.

It was said that she would not cost the College anything. But what of the future? She developed a new and valued activity, so much so that when she later left, there was really no option but to replace her – but this time a salary was needed. So when was the cost incurred? Was it when she left, and a new person had to replace her, or when we first invited her, with all her particular capacities and potential, "at no cost"? That does not mean that we should not have taken her on to the staff in the first place. In her case it was clearly a right decision, but we have to recognize that we must make decisions "not knowing the cost."

On another occasion the circumstances of the teacher taken on at "no cost" changed. Her private income was lost. Could we just say "thank you but good-bye"? We would have had to replace her anyway. Or did we have a responsibility to her that was actually taken on when she was first invited to join the College?

We must be conscious that when we invite any person to join the school, we are taking on possible financial commitments that may not become visible until some time in the future. Destiny works in deep and mysterious ways. These things are not to be seen in the numbers of the accounts, until after they have happened, but they are a cost that is incurred before they can become visible.

There are many such hidden factors in the finances. We have to know what lies behind the figures. This is essential for the making of decisions. To make them purely on the figures, or departmental budgets, will lead to all sorts of unsafe decisions. The only way really to do this, unless she has exceptional capacities, is for the person responsible to be as closely involved as possible in the actual bookkeeping.

If decisions involving expenditure are to be made, not just on the figures in the accounts, but taking into account what lives as "will" and "intention" in the teachers and other colleagues, then those involved with the finances, or at least the central carrier, must be able to sense what it is that lives in her colleagues. For this, the more of the meetings, such as those of the teachers, she can attend, the more efficiently she can work to include in the financial decisions what lives as impulse in the school. She would be in such a meeting as one who listens.

The Dying Organism

A school, like any other community or organization, is a living being. It is born, comes into being, and then grows to maturity. Death forces will enter into it ever more strongly, and eventually it must die. These death forces manifest as a sort of sclerosis that enters into the school. The word "institution" carries in it something of a recognition of these sclerotic tendencies. For many people the word "institution" calls up the concept of a more rigid and less life-endowed establishment than "organization" or "community."

This tendency to sclerosis has constantly to be resisted and overcome. It appears more particularly in the administrative arrangements and procedures and in the defining of functions and responsibilities. A tendency to bureaucracy, to create forms and fixed procedures, will tend to kill initiative and the flexibility needed for growth and change arising out of new ideas. Traditions arise when what was originally thought through and done with clear intention becomes a habit; the reason for it is lost.

It works in many different ways. For instance, it can often happen when one person is in the same work for a long time without change or development; when a person is good at a particular job, for example in reception, she may be left in it for years. After a time there will be no challenge in the work, nothing that re-enlivens it for her, and she begins to do it as a routine, out of habit. Then as the school develops and changes, the office remains the same – it becomes lifeless. This can also be true of long established committees, where there is only an occasional change in the membership.

These hardening tendencies will be there, and in a certain sense they must be there. They are part of growth, but they have constantly and patiently to be resisted and held back.

It is often difficult to see it in one's own school, but when one visits an old and well established school, if one is observant, one can often become aware of much in the organization that is lifeless, that has been unchanged for a long time and is as it is, because that is the way it has always been.

The Development Office

I have a problem with this name. In most schools, as far as I can see, the Development Officer (or Office) is seen as being responsible for the development of the school. By that is meant the raising of the necessary money through appeals and other activities to provide for development of new buildings. It sometimes also includes providing for salaries for new staff and other activities. That itself is, of course, a very necessary work and function. It is the use of the word I question, not the activity. By using this word in this way, it creates the idea that the development of the school is only achieved through the finding of more money and that it takes place in the Development Office. Add to this the fact that it is sometimes suggested that the development officer, responsible for the development of the school, does not need to be particularly familiar or committed to Anthroposophy, though this would be an advantage. Then we have a strange situation.

If development is nothing more than the economic growth of the school, there might be some truth in that. But what about the cultural-spiritual development of the school? What of the development of the inner life and the teaching capacities of the teachers? What of the development in the way meetings are run, and in the working with new young teachers? And if the school decides to work at the questions discussed in this book, is that not development?

By using the word "development" in this way and putting it into an office, the consciousness of the need for spiritual and inner development is suppressed. Without the work in these areas the expansion of the physical body of the school will not be true growth. In my observation this has actually been happening in some schools.

Chapter Twenty-One

A Final Question

The threefold social order is too often thought of in too narrow a sense, as applying basically to the administrative and organizational side of a school or other such community. The teachers are seen as the cultural workers and so should have a certain freedom within which to do their work. The threefold social order is then seen as the task of those in the offices, and possibly including the Board, who should understand the need to separate, and to take responsibility for, the economic - thought of in terms of money, which is always in short supply - and the legal questions.

I hope that this book will have been able, at least to some extent, to have broadened this picture of the threefold social order to one that can be seen only in the context of humanity as a whole, of World Humanity, from which the school is not separate.

The individual school cannot exist as separate from the society of which it is a part. Its very existence, its health and strength, and its possibility of growth can only be a reflection of the state of the society in which it has its being. Whether there are sufficient numbers of people with the inner capacities and freedom to recognize the basis of the teaching and so wish to send their children to the school, whether there is the legal possibility of such an independent school to function in the way it must do, and whether there are the financial resources and the will to make them available to the school, these will all depend on the enlightenment and culture and on the economic and legal circumstances of the wider society of which the school is a part.

What is the present state of this wider society, of world humanity within which the Waldorf schools struggle for existence?

Let us look at the cultural life of today. If we stand in a busy city street or shopping mall, or in the crowd watching some sporting event, we can ask the question: what lives in human souls that is for them an image of their own being, that gives them moral guidance and informs their thinking, feeling and their willing?

If we had stood in such a crowd of people in ancient times and asked the same question, what answer would we then have come to? Would the answer then have been the same as it is today?

I remember once when I visited a town and was told I would see many long faces – the local soccer team had just lost an important match, which they had been expected to win. I had a very vivid imaginative picture of the shame and feeling of loss that was the players, but that was actually experienced by a wide group of people as their own. They were one with the actual players, and the feelings and experience of the team were also that of all, this being also true of very many who had not even been actually present at the game.

We have all experienced something of this, of our belonging to a group, of feeling as the group feels, of being part of a group consciousness. When we experience this, we do so out of a consciousness that really belongs to the past. But such an experience can be a very useful pointer to what worked very much more strongly in ancient times, when the consciousness of self was still very weak.

In those former times what lived in the mystery centers as wisdom radiated outward and, in a certain way, was experienced by the ordinary people as that which gave guidance and purpose to their feelings and their work. Even in the cultural life of the Greeks, the Romans, and into the Middle Ages, though growing progressively weaker, there still spoke through their art, literature, philosophy, and religion sublime truths of the human being's true nature and of his roots in worlds of spirit. These truths lay at the foundation of the life of society in those earlier times.

But today, is it a true picture of the human being that is revealed through so much of our art, that lives there in the teacher, the scientist, the doctor, and even the priest? Do the same sublime truths, which inspired and guided people of former times, still live on in people of today? Where is truth in our time? Is it truth that we see and hear when we watch television or read the paper, when we listen to the politician, or what is said by the world of business? It seems that today instead of the truth, it is all too often untruths and lies that are spread forth.

Our cultural life today, in so far as it is alive, has little ability to inspire a feeling for the truth.

And in rights life? I remember some 50 years ago when I was young and became interested in cars, I was taught that when one came into a village or town where there were street lights, one turned off the headlights of the car and drove on the side-lights. This was so as not to dazzle the other drivers coming towards one.

Then there came a time when this was turned around into the opposite. Then you kept your headlights on so that the other drivers would see you. This was a simple, but for me, revealing manifestation of the change that was coming about; the recognition of the rights of the other person was being transformed into a demand that one's own rights should be properly recognized and provided for.

A rights life that should arise from the recognition that all people are equal, and that the law must apply to all equally, that a person recognizes as valid for others what she expects for herself, has now changed into something of an opposite nature. Now there is a growing tendency to look only to one's own rights, to what is due from others to oneself. This has led to a growing flood of litigation and to a huge increase in insurance due to the need to protect oneself from claims by people standing on their rights. It means also that often a thing that we would like to do, perhaps to help another, we cannot do because we would not be covered by insurance, if something should go wrong and the other person sued us. So we each look after our own interests.

As a judge remarked in a recent case in England, "What has happened to the old fashioned concepts of chance and accident? Now it has always to be someone's fault."

How much further will all this grow and to what sort of human society is it leading us?

And the economic sphere of social life, where is that? As I hope has been shown earlier in this book, it is in the nature of economic life that, through division-of-labor, that is through the development of technology, we now have the possibility of providing for all of humanity. But this is only possible and will happen when in economic life people come to work, not for themselves, but for others, that is when altruism is allowed to hold sway. That is the nature of economic life.

But that which could be the means for providing for all people, so making them free, can instead become that which has power over them. The economic and financial life of the West which was born of the English speaking peoples, first in Great Britain and then taken over by America, which should bring to all the bounty of the earth, instead now spreads its dominion over the whole world.

In December, 1919, Rudolf Steiner gave a lecture in Dornach called "The Mysteries of Light, of Space and of the Earth." He had not been able to travel as planned, and so he gave this extra lecture, the audience of which included quite a number of English friends. In it he traces each sphere of social life to its origins in the mysteries of ancient times. At the end he then looks to the future, to the three abysses that humanity faces if social life is not made threefold:

"... While this stream (cultural life) empties into lies, the middle stream empties into self-seeking, and an economic life like the Anglo-American, which may well end in world-domination if the effort is not made to bring its permeation by the independent spiritual life and the independent political life, will flow into the third of the abysses of human life, into the third of these three."

The first abyss is lies, the degeneration of humanity through Ahriman; the second is self-seeking, the degeneration of humanity through Lucifer; the third is, in the physical realm, illness and death, and in the cultural realm, the illness and death of culture.

"The Anglo-American world may gain world dominion, but without Threefold, the Social Order it will, through this dominion, pour out cultural death and cultural illness over the whole earth; for these are just as much a gift of the Asuras as lies are a gift of Ahriman and self-seeking of Lucifer."

Now, as we arrive at the end of the millennium, if we observe what is happening in the wider social life of humanity, do we not see these three abysses already gaping before us?

Very many years ago, while still in my teens, when reading in the *St. John Gospel*, chapter 15, verses 22 to 24, the thought came very strongly to me, so strongly that I, unusual for me, made a note of it: To what extent does responsibility come with knowledge?

If I come to know that there is a certain danger further down the road, and I see someone going towards it, does the knowledge of the danger place on me an actual responsibility to protect that person, or to warn her? If I do not do so, do I carry some responsibility for what happens?

This is a question that we should take some effort to consider. At the level of the question above, the answer seems obvious. But does responsibility always come with knowledge?

Rudolf Steiner gave a great deal of his time and energy to the question of the threefold social order. Time and again he emphasized its importance for humanity and the fact that it was called for by the evolutionary impulses of our time. He placed before us the knowledge of the threefold nature of human society, just as he did the threefold nature of the human being.

He came to recognize that the people of that time did now yet have the thoughts with which to take hold of it. He speaks of this in the lecture given in April, 1923, of the series *The Cycle of the Year*, given in Dornach.

That was over 70 years ago. Since then there have been enormous changes in human consciousness and human thinking. The widespread increase of awareness of human rights as applying to every human being on this earth is just one example of this. Another is the widespread change in the culture of management in industry, business, and politics. While on one side there has developed ever more strongly the urge to egoism, economic domination, and a quest for wealth, on the other there is an increasing awakening to social questions, a search for new ways of guiding human affairs, as well as an awakening to environmental questions.

Those who know something of the threefold social order and who observe what is happening in fields of management will see that something of this threefold nature is seen, or perhaps more often sensed, and acted upon by an ever increasing number of people. But they do not see the whole. They do not see that it is in the nature of human social life that it has a threefold structure, that each sphere must be separated from the other two in order that each can work according to its own inherent nature, and that only out of the three separated strands can a true unity be found.

But this knowledge has been given by Rudolf Steiner to those of us who recognize Anthroposophy. It is now needed by the world. It is needed by those whose intention it is to bring a healing to social life and who already see something of it.

We must see that many of the problems facing the world, such as unemployment, human rights, the fact of the rich and the poor, environmental problems, and the poverty of culture can only be tackled from a foundation of a threefold society. Indeed, the fact of the absolute necessity of freedom and independence of education from government or economic influence can only be validated by a recognition of the threefold nature of social life.

Further Reading

Rudolf Steiner gave several hundred lectures relating to the Threefold Social Order, as well as writing a book and many articles. In many lectures on other subjects he also gave important insights into the threefold nature of social life. A full list would be too extensive, but the following are some I have found important.

Towards Social Renewal
> (formally published as The Threefold Commonwealth, and also as *The Threefold Social Order*). Book "Die Kernpunkte der Sozialen Fragen," written in 1919.

World Economy
> 14 lectures given in Dornach, July 24 to August 6, 1922.

The Inner Aspect of the Social Question
> 3 lectures given in Zurich - February 4 and 11, and March 9, 1919.

The Social Future
> 6 lectures given in Zürich, October 1919.

Three Oxford Lectures
> Published as *Threefold, The Social Order*, 3 lectures given at a conference on *Spiritual Values in Education and Social Life* in Oxford, England, August 26, 28, and 29, 1922.

The Mysteries of Light, of Space and of the Earth
> A lecture given in Dornach on December 15, 1919.

Anthroposophy and the Social Question
> An essay originally published in "Lucifer-Gnosis" 1906-1908.

Education as a Social Problem
> 6 lectures given in Dornach, August 9-17, 1919.

The Fifth Gospel
> 13 lectures given in Oslo, Berlin and Cologne between October 1, 1913, and February 10, 1914.

The Karma of Vocation
> 10 lectures given in Dornach, November 4-27, 1916.

The Cycle of the Year
> 5 lectures given in Dornach, particularly the two given beginning on Easter Day, April 1-2, 1923.